"Most children believe their fathers are special. This book, Strength in Numbers, shares the author's story of discovering how truly special his father was in overcoming severe challenges to become a champion. From the streets of Philadelphia, through the battlefields of Vietnam, and into the physically demanding world of competitive Judo we share a life story that proves the power of perseverance. It is a power built on the strength of family; tempered in service to country; and proven by conquest of physical handicaps. The picture that emerges is one of a committed family man and a true hero. It's an inspiring story and a story worthy of being shared."

Dr. Ray Young
Associate Vice President and Dean of Learner Services,
Thomas Edison State College, Trenton, New Jersey.
Lieutenant Colonel, United States Marine Corps (Retired)

"Strength in Numbers is an inspirational memoir of one man's journey from the battlefields of Vietnam, to adapting to everyday life as a disabled veteran, and eventually becoming a Judo champion. It is easy for me to relate to the author's childhood fascination with his father's experiences during Vietnam because I was also raised in a household that was effected by war. My father and uncle both served with the Army and fought in Vietnam. My father made it back but my uncle, Clayton Eugene Fraley, was killed by small arms fire on March 6, 1969. This book portrays the true meaning of adversity and it is a must read."

Hank Fraley
National Football League, Center/Guard 2000-2011
Offensive Line Coach: University of San Diego, 2012-2013
San Jose State University, 2013-present

"Strength in Numbers" is the true story of the life of Joe Walters, a man who persevered through difficult and painful circumstances, and with the support of his family and friends went on to achieve great success. Joe's support network also referred to as the "team", helped him cope with life threatening injuries resulting from combat and the subsequent memories. They encouraged him to pursue his goals and excel in the sport he loved so much. This book will inspire anyone who has ever faced seemingly insurmountable adversity, but with the support of a loving "team", worked through their difficulties, past the pain, and achieved greatness. Joe Walters refused to allow himself to be defined by his physical challenges and went on to become a champion in judo. Joe's inspirational story as told by his son, Joseph F. Walters, is well worth the read.

Jon Runyan
Congressman, New Jersey
3rd Congressional District
National Football League: Offensive Tackle 1996-2009

STRENGTH IN NUMBERS

by

Joseph F. Walters

Author's Note

Everything that is written in this book is true and is recounted from the best of my father's memory. With that being said, the dialogue may not be word for word, but the basis of what is being said is accurate.

Acknowledgments

I have been assisted in this endeavor by a host of great family members and friends who provided their support and guidance while this book was being completed. I would like to gratefully acknowledge:

My wonderful and supportive wife, Alicia Walters; my loving mother, Beth Walters; my sister, Alison Stevens; my brother-in-law, James Stevens; my father-in-law, Gil Segal; and my mother-in-law, Susan Segal.

I would like to give a special thanks to the following people for the behind-the-scenes work they put into making this project become reality:

To William Henry, for your rough editing of the original manuscript. I know the whole process was very time-consuming, and I am forever grateful for your assistance.

To my attorney, Avery Teitler, for providing me with great legal advice and assistance during this whole process.

To Jeff Pierson Jr., for all the hard work you put into designing the original outline, cover and interior of this book. You are a talented graphic artist, and I know that you have a bright future in this field.

To Matt Reeves, for your great networking skills and for your tireless pursuit of getting the original manuscript read by the right people.

Last but not least, I would like to thank my father. Dad, you are and will forever be my hero. I hope I did your story justice. It is time for the rest of the world to learn what you have always instilled in me—that there is always strength in numbers.

This book is dedicated to my daughter, Aubrey Walters, and my nephew, Jackson Stevens. This is your pop pop's life story. He is a living testament. I hope the two of you are able to learn from his experiences and see that, with strong will, determination, and the guidance of others, there is no hardship that can't be overcome.

Chapter 1 · My Hero

I was eight years old when I first realized that my father was different from the other dads. This realization occurred more than two decades ago, but it is still fresh in my mind, as if it happened yesterday. I recall that it was a scorching hot day in July of 1986, and I was playing baseball with some friends in a schoolyard in my hometown.

I was your average South Jersey kid. I loved the Philadelphia Phillies, and Pete Rose was my hero. When I say hero, I mean a god! "Charlie Hustle," "Run it out like Pete"—this is all that I heard that summer at the baseball field: fathers telling their young sons to play baseball like Pete. This was a guy who would sprint to first base when he was walked and wouldn't think twice about diving headfirst into a catcher, even after his helmet had fallen off. Even though Peter Edward Rose was no longer playing for the Phillies, all of the children, including myself, wanted to be just like him.

On this day, as I approached the plate, I dug into the batter's box, kicking my foot back and forth across the ground. As a small dirt cloud rose around me, I banged my aluminum baseball bat on top of the plate, and I could feel its strong vibration reach my fingertips. When I looked up to face the pitcher, I noticed that all the other kids were staring in the opposite direction, fixated on a small hill that was attached to the school. The sun was directly in my eyes, so it took a few seconds before I realized that our baseball game had been interrupted because of my father. He was wearing a twenty-five-pound weighted vest and was hopping up and down the hill. One of the kids then turned to me with a look of confusion on his face and asked, "Joey, what is your dad doing?" Without hesitation, I answered, "Oh, he's just training. He's got a judo competition coming up." I knew what the next question was going to be, and, before anyone could ask, I continued, "He got shot in the war. That's why he has only one leg." Another kid then chimed in, "Yeah, my dad calls your dad the one-legged judo champion, and he says that he's some kind of hero." I didn't know what to say, so I just nodded in agreement and shouted at the pitcher, "Just throw the ball."

After the game, I approached my father. He was now sitting on the hill, staring intently toward a wooded area located behind the school. Even though his workout had been over for some time, he was still sweating profusely. When I approached him, he jumped, as if he was startled, and said, "I'm sorry, Joey. I guess I was daydreaming." I asked, "Daydreaming about what?" He hesitated for a short while before answering. "Joey, sometimes I am reminded of some bad things that happened in my past. I don't want to remember these things, but for some reason the memories will not go away. Someday you will understand, but I pray to God each and every day that your eyes will never see the horrors I have lived through." As I tried to comprehend what he was talking about, I could tell he was still distracted by whatever he had seen in the woods. I asked, "Dad, what did you see out there?" He turned to me with a serious look on his face and replied, "Sometimes I see the shadows of the enemy and the shadows of the friends who I have lost."

At the time, I could not understand the true meaning of what my father was talking about. However, while sitting on the hill with him, it became evident that there was more to his life than just being my father. That other part of his life was Vietnam, and, up until that day, he had never spoken about his experiences during the war. It was as if he had put the past behind him and just wanted to move on with life.

But how could he move on? He was missing his left leg from the knee down, and he was now garnering local media attention because of his judo accomplishments. It also didn't help that every article written about him always retold the same story of his past, focusing on the Vietnam War. I guess being dubbed the "one-legged judo hero" didn't help either. In any case, he would never reveal specific details about the war. He would just acknowledge that he had been shot by enemy gunfire while serving with the Marine Corps in Vietnam. That was it, and people would always seem surprised that despite what he had been through, he seemed somewhat normal.

But was he? Especially after this conversation on the hill, I really wasn't sure. How do you explain to your eight-year-old son that you just had a flashback of Vietnam? At the time, I couldn't imagine what he was talking about, and, looking back now, it really confused the hell out of me. I think he just wanted to forget the war and get on with living a normal life.

But was it normal to pick up a seventy-five-pound boulder and throw it across your front yard while standing on one leg? Then drop down to the ground and knock out several sets of push-ups? This wasn't something the other fathers did in my neighborhood, but I had watched him train like this my entire life. I was probably the only kid in the entire world who had a one-legged national judo champion as a father. So, I realized it was fair to say that my father was not like the other dads, and he was definitely not normal.

That scorching hot day in July was a day of firsts and lasts. It marked the first time my father spoke to me about his experiences in Vietnam, and it was the last time he mentioned the war until three years later, when I was eleven years old. Then, just like the first time, his willingness to speak occurred as a result of a flashback. However, this flashback was not triggered by a thickly wooded tree line that resembled Vietnam. This flashback was brought on by modern-day cinema.

Chapter 2 • War Movies

I know it is normal for most American boys to fantasize about war, but for me it was more of an obsession. I can remember going to bed at night and, while trying to go to sleep, thinking about fighting in Vietnam. In my mind I would be calling in artillery, setting up ambushes, and single-handedly shooting as many Viet Cong as possible. I realize this doesn't seem normal, and you're probably wondering why a father would teach his eleven-year-old son about combat. But don't blame my father; at this point he would still not talk about the war, so I was left with only one choice for conducting my research. Basically, you can blame John Rambo and Colonel James Braddock for first teaching me about Vietnam.

I began my research with Rambo: First Blood Part II, starring Sylvester Stallone, and Missing in Action and Missing in Action 2: The Beginning, starring Chuck Norris. To an eleven-year-old kid, these two fictional characters were larger than life. They had both been prisoners of war and were brutally tortured by the Viet Cong. They also both returned years later in search of fellow POWs and to wreak havoc on their one-time captors. I idolized these guys, and I often wondered if my own father was a hero like them. These movies also filled a void, because my father was still very tightlipped about his experiences during the war. Even though I watched these movies on a daily basis, he would never join me. He would just jokingly ask, "How many bad guys did Rambo take out with his knife today?" or "Did Chuck kick those bad guys all the way back to Cambodia?"

Even then, I knew that these films were exaggerated tales of combat, but I think they gave me just enough knowledge so I could carry on a conversation with him about Vietnam. We would talk about the rugged terrain, the horrendous bugs, and the fact that he slept almost every night on the ground. (I guess I know now why he never took me camping.) But the one thing these movies did not explain to me was what my father had mentioned during the flashback three years earlier at the baseball field. No matter how many times I watched these films, I could never find out the meaning of what he'd said: "Sometimes I see the shadows of the enemy." So when I finally gathered enough courage and asked him to explain about the shadows, he remained quiet for a short while and replied, "When I think you're ready, I will show you."

About six months later, my father woke me from a sound sleep and said, "Get up. I need to show you something." So, without hesitation, I wiped the crust from my eyes and joined him in the living room. When I entered the room and noticed empty beer cans on the table next to his beloved La-Z-Boy chair, I wasn't surprised. I never considered him an alcoholic, but it was no secret that on weekends he enjoyed staying up late to watch old movies and drink beer. But the real surprise came when he pushed Play on the VCR, and the movie Platoon appeared on the television screen.

I had already overheard my mother telling one of her girlfriends that my father had gone alone to watch it at the movie theater but left halfway through. She said that apparently he wasn't ready to relive the war, and that he couldn't sleep for days after watching just half of the movie. My mother's comments made me very curious, but I was eleven years old, and this was not a PG-rated film. So whenever I asked her if we could rent Platoon, she would smile and say, "Just stick with your Rambo movies for now."

As the movie played, I could not keep my eyes off my father. I studied his every move, and he was mentioning things that he had never said before (I'm sure because of the beer he had consumed). During combat scenes, he would turn to me and say, "Joey, those guys better get closer to the ground," or "Right now would be a good time to throw a hand grenade," or "Those guys have to keep on moving." I could see his facial expressions change from scene to scene, and for the first time, I realized why he never hesitated to make fun of Rambo. And how could he not? In this movie, the soldiers were not afraid to show emotion. Almost every character displayed fear, pain, and rage. They worked together to accomplish a goal, and it made my favorite Vietnam movies seem so far-fetched. As I was sitting there with him, I could not stop smiling. I was proud that he had decided to share this experience with me, and it was a true bonding moment between father and son. But just like the old saying, "all good things must come to an end," our end came without warning. During one scene in particular, he shut off the movie, mumbled a few words, and after a long silence, said, "I think it is time for you to go back to bed. We have both seen too much tonight."

I didn't argue with him or ask any questions. But that evening, I stayed up most of the night thinking about the scene that made him shut off the movie. This part was not necessarily violent, but for some reason it really affected his demeanor. In the scene, the main character, Chris Taylor (played by Charlie Sheen), is set up on a night ambush. He has just woken up, and as he is wiping bugs and dirt from his face, he looks out into the distance. The only thing you can see is thick brush and vegetation, but suddenly the foliage starts to move very slowly. And it was at this moment that my father leaned forward in his chair and began to push his fingers together. He looked very intense, so I asked, "What are you doing with your fingers? What is wrong?" He didn't answer. As the shadow moved closer, you could now see the outline of a North Vietnamese soldier approaching the ambush site. I'm not sure what happened next, because this is where my father shut off the movie. And immediately after switching off the movie, he mumbled something under his breath. I didn't hear the whole thing, but I did make out something about a "claymore mine." Then it dawned on me that when my father was pushing his fingers together, in his mind, he was trying to activate the claymore mines — the claymore mines that Charlie Sheen's character was having trouble trying to set off and the same mines that would have easily killed the enemy soldier who was trying to sneak into the ambush site.

I guess my father was right: maybe I had seen too much. Because that evening, I finally understood what he meant when he said, "Sometimes I see the shadows of the enemy." He was referring to the shadow of the enemy soldier, just like in Platoon, creeping into the ambush site. This was probably the same shadow he had seen a hundred times in Vietnam and, years later, in his worst nightmares. It was the same shadow that forced him to have another flashback of the war, the second one I had witnessed in a three-year period.

This was a humbling experience for me, because I was raised watching my father train and compete in the sport of judo. Even though he had only one leg, he was a fierce competitor, and he often put his own body through hell just to win. He was my Pete Rose, and I was proud of the fact that every kid thought I was a judo expert just like him. No one ever really messed with me, and when he was training for a competition, it was as if Rocky Balboa was living in our house. But, watching him become emotional and visibly distraught because of a movie, I realized that my fascination with the Vietnam War had to end. It wasn't healthy for my father to go through this, and I felt guilty for pressuring him into dealing with his past, especially after he had done such a good job putting the bad stuff behind him and moving on with his life.

So for the next seventeen years, I kept my promise to myself.
No matter how hard it was, I did not mention Vietnam to him again.
As time went on, I grew from that nosey eleven-year-old kid into
an adult. But I never stopped being curious about Vietnam, and,
when I was twenty-eight years old, my father finally broke his
silence about the war.

Chapter 3 · Cancer

In November 2006, my mother broke the news to me that my father had been diagnosed with prostate cancer. The news was devastating, but deep down I knew he would pull through. I mean, how could he not? He was in great shape, and even though he was no longer competing in judo, he still worked out twice a day. He had always maintained a high level of physical fitness by doing extreme cardiovascular workouts and eating a well-balanced diet. It was all part of his daily routine, and it is ironic to think that after all those years of maintaining a healthy lifestyle, cancer could still sneak in without warning.

After hearing the news, I immediately went to look for him. I had a good idea of where to look, and it didn't take long for me to find him. When I pulled into the parking lot of the elementary school, I noticed him standing on top of the hill that was attached to the school. He was wearing what I like to refer to as his post-Vietnam uniform: a Marine Corps sweatshirt and a Third Battalion, Fifth Marines, baseball cap. When I approached him, I saw that he was out of breath, and as he wiped the sweat from his brow, he said, "I guess Mom told you. I have prostate cancer. The doctors are optimistic that it hasn't spread, but I am going to need surgery. After everything I have been through, I never expected this bump in the road. But in my lifetime, I have been to hell and back. This isn't going to knock me down, and I am ready to fight."

I guess it is fair to say that when most people make arrangements for surgery, there is really no preparation. After various tests and meetings with doctors, you just show up to the hospital on your assigned date and go under the knife. It appeared that my father's game plan was different. He was preparing for surgery as if he were going into battle.

As I was walking back to my vehicle, I turned around and asked, "Why did you return to this hill? What about the shadows?" He smiled and replied, "I didn't think you still remembered. That was a long time ago. But as I tried to tell you then, the shadows of the enemy and the friends that I have lost will always be with me. So just remember, regardless if it is good or bad, there is always strength in numbers."

When I got back to my vehicle, I beeped the horn to get his attention. He then turned in my direction, raised his fist in the air, and once again shouted, "Strength in numbers!" As I drove off, I glanced in the rearview mirror and watched him hop down the hill to the jungle gym, jump up to one of the bars, and then knock out a set of pull-ups.

After speaking with him, it was hard not to get emotional. He was facing potentially life-threatening surgery, and he had returned to this hill to gather his physical and inner strength. Also, that hill evoked a long-forgotten memory from my childhood: a baseball game, that same hill, and the first time I realized that my father was not like the other dads. I guess it was fair to say that after all those years, my father was still not normal.

Chapter 4 · I Have Been Here Before

As the nurse wheeled my father down the hallway, our eyes met, and he shot me a quick wink. At that moment, I was overcome with a huge sense of relief because he had survived the surgery. He looked very weak and was somewhat dazed from the anesthesia, but he had pulled through. As I sat with him, I could tell that he was in severe discomfort, but he would not show any pain because his family was with him. My sister, Alison, had flown in from Pittsburgh, and along with my mother and my wife, Alicia, we were all at his bedside. The doctor deemed his surgery a success, and we were informed that he would be spending two more days in the hospital for recovery.

As two days grew into three and then four, his condition began to worsen. On the fourth day, I was in the hospital room alone with him while he was taking a nap. When he awoke, he scanned the room to ensure that my mother was not present and said, "Joey, this doesn't look good. They have to stop the bleeding, or I am going to—" He stopped before finishing the sentence, but I knew exactly what he was trying to say. Up until that moment, I was under the impression that he was just having some minor complications. I didn't know that he was thinking about death. He then whispered, "I have been here before." I asked, "Been where?" At that moment, his doctor entered the room, and our conversation ended. After a brief examination, the doctor advised that the bleeding had stopped, and that his vital signs were improving. This news was a huge relief, and we were now able to focus on getting him released from the hospital. Prior to leaving his room for the evening, I said to him, "Enough is enough: you have some explaining to do, and I want to know everything." He asked, "Everything?" And I answered, "Yeah, everything about your past. Vietnam, judo—I want to hear everything." He smiled and said, "Your past is kind of like a book. You have to start by reading the beginning in order to truly understand the end. So if you want to learn about my past, I must first tell you about the path I traveled to get to Vietnam and the people who helped me get there—the same people who first showed me the concept of strength in numbers."

That evening in the hospital room, my father spoke briefly about the beginning portion of his life. Don't get me wrong: I had always heard stories of his childhood, especially the good times he shared with his family and friends. So when I asked him, "What about the good stuff? Is Vietnam next?" He laughed and replied, "Soon, very soon. Be patient and wait till I get out of this hospital, because you will understand very shortly that I have spent enough time in hospitals to last a lifetime."

So a few weeks later, I sat down with him in the living room of his house. I was armed with nothing more than a pen and paper; the time had finally come for me to learn everything about his past, specifically Vietnam. My father seemed nervous, and after settling into his beloved La-Z-Boy, he made one point clear before he would begin speaking about his past. He instructed me that a certain part of his life could be told only by him. He said, "You can't speak about combat unless you experienced it firsthand. These memories, even the ones that haunt me each and every day of my life, are sacred to me. My words represent the men who died under my command and the person I once was.

Because that innocent and free-loving kid I used to be was left behind on the battlefield and does not exist anymore, the only reminder I have of him is my words. So the point I am trying to make is that if you ever write about my life experiences, that time period has to be presented in my spoken words."

Basically, the following is written from the pen of a son, but directly from the spoken words of my father. After ironing out his list of demands, my father began by taking a deep breath and blurting out, "Believe it or not, Joey, it all began with a short run."

Chapter 5 · Vietnam: June 1968

When I started to run, I immediately noticed that I was not in the same physical condition that I had been a few months prior. It had been a few weeks since my last workout, and I guess all the travel time and the administrative process just to get there had caught up to me. It was hard to breathe, and the air was so humid, my lungs felt like they were on fire. I had run for only about twenty seconds when suddenly a young Marine jumped in my path and shouted, "Lieutenant, you're going to get yourself killed. What in the hell are you doing?" I answered, "I'm just going for a short run." The Marine looked no more that eighteen years old, and he actually resembled a guy who I knew from the Jersey Shore. When he stopped me, I could tell that he was confused, and with that he said, "Charlie"—which is the surname used when referring to the Viet Cong—"is in that village over there, and he can snipe at us at any time. As soon as you do something different, you set yourself up as a target. Your short run could have been a short death." Although I was somewhat embarrassed, I thanked him for his advice. I also realized that in spite of all the firepower at our disposal, the enemy in this case had home-field advantage. As I walked back to my hooch, which was another name for our living quarters, I began to reflect on the sights I had witnessed since arriving in Vietnam.

When my plane arrived in Da Nang, the first thing I saw was a sign that read Welcome to Vietnam. I also observed pallets of caskets waiting to be sent home. When I stepped off the plane, I was immediately taken aback by the odor that emanated from the "grave registration" area located across from the check-in center. This area stunk like nothing I had smelled before. It was a putrid and disgusting odor that, unfortunately, I would soon be forced to smell quite often. The odor I'm referring to is the smell of death.

After I retrieved my personal belongings, I was informed that I would be transported to a smaller base the following day, and that I should take the time to enjoy the amenities that this base had to offer. Da Nang was a sprawling Marine base camp that you could compare to a small town. Enemy attacks were very rare, and the only sound of war you heard was the occasional siren or the roar of jeeps as they passed by.

Joe Walters - An Hoa Base Camp

I hadn't had a haircut for a while, so I stopped at the base barbershop for a quick trim. The Vietnamese barber working at the shop seemed nice, but when he walked across the room and picked up a straight razor, I started to feel very uncomfortable. As he started to use the razor to shape my

sideburns, I couldn't help but think how easy it would be for him to just reach down and slice it across my neck. I also wondered if he was one of the many Viet Cong who worked on the base during the day and would shoot at the Marines at night. Of one thing I'm sure: when I walked out of the barbershop, it was the last time I allowed any Vietnamese to come near me with a sharp object.

The following day I arrived in An Hoa, which was the battalion combat base just southwest of Da Nang. It was a fairly large base in the middle of nowhere that contained a small airstrip. When I arrived, the company was out on operations, and I had to wait several days before I would be able to join them. I was instructed that I would be assigned to the Third Battalion, Fifth Marines, Mike Company; from what I had been told, they were involved in fierce combat in an area referred to as the Arizona Territory, branded such because it resembled the rugged and hostile badlands of the American Southwest. It was flat, low-lying terrain, where a lot of Marines lost their lives.

I spent the next five days at An Hoa, and other than the embarrassing "running incident," those days were uneventful. I spent most of my time reading and just trying to mentally prepare for whatever lay ahead. On day six, I heard a rumor that my company would be returning from the field. I was relieved, but at the same time, I was scared as hell. It was now evident that I would be trading the comforts of this base for the rough and rugged terrain of war.

That evening I went to get chow at the mess hall, which was nothing but a plywood shack. I sat down next to another lieutenant who had been at An Hoa for a while, and even before I could introduce myself, he blurted out, "This worthless piece of land is a hot spot for fighting. Do you see that village over there? Well, the local Viet Cong can fire on us almost at will, while the ones in the bush take great pleasure in sending rockets and mortars just to let you know that they are there. You don't know this yet, but most of the actual fighting takes place in the area called the Basin. It is heavily fortified with numer-

ous tree lines, trenches, tunnels, and spider holes. The NVA [North Vietnamese Army] can appear out of nowhere and attack us at their convenience. Then they just as easily disappear back into the ground to get some rest and wait for another day." He was staring off toward the village in a complete daze, and he was rambling on so much that I couldn't eat my food. He looked like he had been through hell, and I couldn't help noticing that both of his legs slightly trembled while he spoke. I tried to change the subject by asking where he was from, but he completely ignored me and continued, "Most of the men are highly trained NVA regulars who work with the hardcore VC. Their main purpose in life is to kill Marines, and they love it. Our damn battalion has taken too many casualties over the past year, and it is slowly getting worse. More than half of the officers have been wounded or killed, and the enlisted men only wonder when it's their turn to step on a mine or get shot by a 'friendly' villager from that cesspool over there. I don't even like to get to know the men, because as soon as you do they—" And with that he stood up and quietly said, "Lieutenant, I have said enough. At times, I don't know when to keep my mouth shut. I have been here a long time, and I really miss my family." He started to walk away, but for some reason he stopped dead in his tracks and said, "Lieutenant, you're not alone." As he began to exit the room, he mumbled three words that I will never forget, and at the time I did not understand: "Strength in numbers."

Joe Walters (Center) · Jim Quinn (Right)

I had just started to eat my food when I overheard another Marine say that Mike Company was back on base. Standing up, I took a deep breath and told myself to remain calm. I left the mess hall and saw the company standing outside the barbed-wire fence and clearing their weapons. At the same time, one of the men was walking slowly toward my location. After making eye contact with him, he suddenly spun around and shouted, "Double-check and make sure there are no rounds in your chambers. You know what happened last time." He turned to me and said, "Lieutenant Walters, my name is Captain Pacello. We just got back from the Arizona Territory, and I am sure glad to see you." I was taken by surprise that he knew who I was, and when he recognized my surprise, he said, "I was told by one of the men on the supply helicopter that you were here." He then pointed to my shirt, which displayed my name tag, and we both began to laugh. I felt like an idiot.

Captain Frank Pacello was about six feet tall and could not have weighed more than 130 pounds. However, his slender stature was not a factor because, as I would soon witness firsthand, the men were more afraid of him than of the enemy. He was of Italian descent, with a fiery temper. He had arrived in Vietnam in 1967 and spent a short time with the First Marine Division, until the company commander of Mike Company was wounded during the Tet Offensive. I had already heard on base that he displayed a special talent for fighting the enemy, and he would not hesitate to advance to the sound of gunfire.

Frank Pacello

After the meeting with Captain Pacello, I decided to return to my hooch to get my gear ready and try to get some rest. I knew that we would be moving out from the base camp shortly, and this would probably be the last time that I would get the opportunity to sleep with a roof over my head. While lying in my bunk, I began to think about my family and the fact that I might not ever see them again. It was hard not to get emotional, but at that moment I realized that, theoretically, I was already dead. The horrible sights I witnessed at grave registration were still fresh on my mind. It also dawned on me that when my tour was over, I would be leaving Vietnam in the same manner that I had arrived: by plane. But would I be sitting in the passenger section, sipping a cold beer, or would I be in the rear of the plane inside of a body bag? From that moment on, I made a pact with myself that it was just easier to think I was already dead. I know that sounds extremely morbid, but I had a job to do, and the fear of death was too overwhelming. But thinking that I was already dead was the easy part. The hard part was remembering that I was a Marine Corps Officer who was going to lead men into combat. Just the thought of that was mind-blowing, and it made me feel nauseated. I mean, is anyone ever ready for that task?

I know Captain Pacello sure looked like a leader, especially when I saw him addressing his men. Admittedly he was authoritative, but the Marines listened to every word that came out of his mouth—not just because they had to, but because it seemed they all knew that his words would eventually keep them out of harm's way. And the more I thought about it, the more I began to question if I was in over my head. Who the hell was I? I had no combat experience, and I was now going to be leading a bunch of Marines, who I didn't even know, into battle. Although I was a graduate of the Marine Corps Officer Candidate School, which was no easy task, the average Marine, especially the ones who were fighting in Vietnam, was still leery of you until you gained his trust. My first goal was to prove myself to them, and this wasn't going to be an easy task, because all of them had already seen combat. So, basically, I was the new guy. The new twenty-seven-year-old second lieutenant who was now going to lead a bunch of eighteen- and nineteen-year-old kids through hell. It was crucial that I prove to the men that I was a capable leader, and, most importantly, that I was not going to lead them to their untimely deaths. I knew that I was ready for the challenge, but I wanted an answer right then and there. Am I ready for this? Am I going to be a good leader? How will I react when the real stuff hits the fan? The more questions I asked myself, the more nervous I became. I was breathing heavily, and I was starting to sweat. Finally, I said to myself, "Just calm down, and knock off all the crap. You're ready for this. You can do this. Just think about everything you went through to get here—all of the hard work and all of the struggles you overcame." And at that point, I began to think about my past and the fact that most people, including myself at times, thought I would never amount to anything. I was a real screwup, and, boy, did I make some dumb mistakes when I was young. It was hard not to laugh, because if my Catholic schoolteachers only knew that I was now in the position to lead men into combat, they would be saying prayer after prayer. But they wouldn't be praying on my behalf; they would be praying for my men. But how could I blame them? Because while growing up, I was the furthest thing from a Marine you could find—I was a Walters.

Chapter 6 · Joseph Edmund Walters

I was born on January 8, 1941, in the Mount Airy section of Philadelphia, Pennsylvania. My father, Raymond Walters, owned a plumbing and heating business, and he was a product of the generation that survived World War I, the Great Depression, World War II, and the Korean War. My father had been in the army during the First World War, but he was fortunate not to experience any combat. By the time World War II came around, he was too old and had too many children to go back into the service. I guess it is fair to say that living through such critical times enabled my parents to appreciate life and, most importantly, enjoy

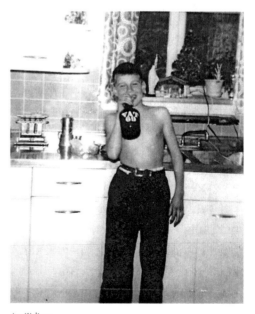

Joe Walters

spending time with their family. My mother, Caroline, was born in South Philadelphia, and she met my father through mutual friends. She was a stay-at-home housewife and spent most of her time just trying to stay ahead of her seven children.

My brothers—Raymond, Billy, Dick, Charlie, and John—were all hell-raisers, and we were known in our neighborhood for our fighting abilities. We did not go around town starting fights, but if someone messed with us, we didn't hesitate to throw punches. I was a very skinny kid, but because of my four older brothers, I learned to take a punch at an early age. Raymond and Billy were much older, and John was a few years younger, so I spent most of my childhood cruising the streets with Dick and Charlie. Dick was one tough son of a gun. He was born with above-average strength, and he had the street smarts to size up a situation very quickly. I never saw Dick start a fight, but on many occasions I witnessed him drop someone, or multiple people, with little difficulty.

I can remember those times when a fight was about to break out. The crowd would just start to gather around, and you could feel your nerves jumping out of your skin. I hated being in those situations; deep down, I knew that I could never back down. It was just something you did to prove your manhood, and every kid, at some point in life, experiences this. But when Dick was in those situations, he showed no fear. He almost seemed to relax just before a fight. There was a certain calmness that came over him, and I could remember

Dick Walters

always feeling sorry for the other guy. Even though the other guy probably provoked the fight and deserved whatever he had coming his way, I knew that Dick was going to show no mercy. As always, someone from the crowd would yell, "Fight!" And within a millisecond, Dick would transition from calmness to complete insanity. It was as if a light switch flipped in his head. It was scary to witness, and God forbid if someone else tried to jump in, because they would now be entangled in Dick's web. He didn't care how much bigger or how much older his opponents were; Dick would never quit. No matter how badly he was beaten, he would just fight until the other guy gave up. And when the fight was over, Dick would lean over the guy, reach out his hand, and help him up off the ground. That was the kind of kid Dick was, and thank God he was always on my side.

Dick Walters · Joe Walters · Charlie Walters · John Walters
Raymond Walters · Raymond Walters Sr.

Charlie was the complete opposite of Dick. Charlie was the happy-go-lucky type, and he did his best to avoid physical altercations.

Dick Walters · John Walters · Joe Walters

Charlie was everyone's friend, and he loved to have a good time.
But sometimes, people would confuse Charlie's kindness as being
a weakness. And then Charlie would be forced to do something that
he often avoided—fight. You see, Charlie didn't just fight; he could
pulverize someone with just one punch. Charlie had that knockout
punch that most boxing instructors couldn't teach. It wasn't necessarily

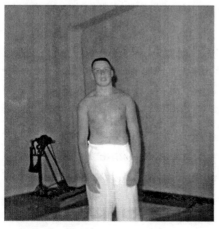

Joe Walters (17 years old)

instinctual; it was more raw power
than anything else. Charlie hit like
a truck, and I always did whatever
I could to avoid being on the other
end of his fist. But, as I previously
mentioned, I made some dumb
mistakes when I was kid, and one
of those mistakes happened in
Charlie's presence. I had gotten
into a heated argument with my
mother and for some reason,

I directed a curse word toward her. I'm not sure what I said exactly, but it was a terrible mistake. Because, the next thing I knew, I was lying on the kitchen floor, and Charlie was standing over me, saying, "Don't you ever talk to Mom like that again." I was out of line, and I definitely deserved having my clock cleaned. I just wished that it had been one of my other brothers who overheard the argument, because my head hurt for days.

I also had a younger sister named Caroline, who was just as tough as her brothers. She was the only girl in our family, and because of this, she learned at an early age how to defend herself. When she was a child, she picked up the nickname Butchie, due to her tomboy persona. She was a tough girl, but beyond her nickname, Butchie was the glue that held our family together. Butchie helped my mother with all the household chores, and she always made sure that her six brothers were well fed and had clean clothes on their backs. She was equivalent to having a second mother, and because of this, I think that she missed out on a great deal of her childhood. While the other girls were going to dances and chasing boys, Butchie was at home, taking care of her family. There is no doubt in my mind that the personal sacrifices Butchie made for our family helped make my and my brothers' childhoods somewhat easier. In my case, I needed all the help that I could get.

I had a decent childhood, but I struggled immensely in school. And when I say struggle, I mean that I really struggled. It wasn't that I was a bad kid; I just don't think I conformed too well to the Catholic school environment. The Catholic nuns were always threatening to fail me, but for some reason they never did. I wasn't sure if it was because they liked me, or that the classes were just too large. It may have been because my father always gave a generous donation when they needed it most. It was probably a combination of all three elements, but I would prefer to think that they were just trying to help push me along. Either way, it didn't make a difference, because when I got to high school, I really screwed things up for myself.

I started the ninth grade at Roosevelt Junior High School, and, after several months, my entire family moved from Mount Airy to Springfield, Montgomery County, Pennsylvania. I hated going to a new school, especially because my years of just getting by finally caught up with me. When I arrived at the new school, they immediately put me back from the ninth to the eighth grade. Because of this, I rebelled and did as little schoolwork as possible. At the end of the school year, I failed miserably, and while my other siblings were at our shore house in Ocean City, New Jersey, I was attending summer school. I may be the only person to ever pass and then fail the eighth grade.

The following fall, I started the ninth grade for the second time in my life. As usual, academics were not my strong point, and I failed the ninth grade. On the last day of school, I rushed home, because I knew that I was in serious trouble. When I got to my house, I approached my father, who was working in our garage. I vividly remember thinking, "I am such a screwup. How the hell am I going to explain this? What an idiot." I then walked up to him and said, "Pop, I have something to show you." I was really scared, petrified that he was going to lose his mind or, even worse, get my brother Charlie to punch me. Basically, my report card went over like a lead balloon. When my father began to read the card, I watched his facial expression change from one of contentment to one of great concern. The thing that bothered me the most was that he wouldn't even look at me or say anything at all. He just stood there and stared at the card with a bewildered look on his face. Finally, after what seemed like an eternity, he asked, "Son, what am I going to do with you?" He then pulled me close, gave me a huge hug, and said, "Don't worry about this setback. I know that you and schoolwork have never mixed too well. We will get through this together, and I will figure something out. Now get out of here and go play with your friends."

I realize that my academic deficiencies certainly disheartened my father. But the way he handled this situation was a true testament of his character. Even though most parents would have punished their children for this type of behavior, my father responded with love and support. My father knew that I couldn't have cared less about school, but he had six other children to worry about, and we were all well aware of his plans for our future. My father always stressed to my brothers and me that we were either going to college, a trade school, or into the military. Although I was royally screwing things up for myself, I knew my father would support me just as long I followed his future game plan. But, after failing the eighth grade twice and the ninth grade once, I was heading down a path for personal destruction. I was still a somewhat decent kid, but I was starting to feel like an outcast among my friends and family. At the time, I don't think they realized that I didn't like being known as the screwup, the dumb kid in the class, and the troublemaker. Because in actuality, I knew I was capable of doing the schoolwork. It wasn't rocket science, but in the past I never had a reason to succeed. It was just easier to sit in class and stare out the window. My future was now heading toward a pivotal crossroad, and I knew that I had to straighten myself out. The rite of passage was over, and it was time to make my father proud.

The following school year, I changed my ways. I completed my home-work, paid attention in class, and passed most of my examinations. I still slacked off as much as I could, but I made a pact with myself that I was never going to fail a grade again. I was still far behind my peers, and I put in only just enough effort to pass my courses. I know it sounds pitiful, but it was a start in the right direction, and for the first time in my life, I couldn't wait to show my father my report card. I knew that he was going to be so proud of my progress, and the thought of seeing him smile while looking at the card was my motivation. But, unfortunately, I would never be able to share this moment with him, because before the school year ended, my father died of heart failure.

After my father's death, our entire family relocated to Ocean City, New Jersey. By this time, most of my siblings were moving in separate directions. Raymond was working for the Philadelphia Plumber's

Union; Charlie was in the US Navy; Billy and Dick were in the US
Marine Corps; John was still just a kid; and Butchie had dropped out
of high school to take care of our mother. Even though I had been doing
better in school, my grades plummeted after my father passed away.
I guess you could say that after he died, I had no reason to care
anymore. I gave up on myself, and school was the last place I wanted
to be. It even got so bad that during my senior year of high school I was
told that I was not going to graduate. At that specific moment, I realized
that I was a true screwup. I was out of options, and I knew that I was
not going to do another year of school, especially after all my friends
graduated. I had to come up with a plan, and, after much consideration,
I made a deal with my teachers. The deal was that if they allowed me
to graduate, I would immediately join the army. Miraculously, that
spring, I was somehow able to pass every course. Well, I don't think I
technically passed every course—my teachers basically did whatever
they could (right or wrong) to help me graduate. Either way, after high
school, I lived up to my word and immediately joined the US Army.

Chapter 7 · The Army

In 1959, I attended basic training
at Fort Benning, Georgia. After basic,
I completed Advanced Infantry Training
and eventually went to Jump School
to be an Army Paratrooper. After Jump
School, I was assigned to Fort Bragg,
North Carolina, with the Eighty-Second
Airborne, Second 501st Battle Group.
During my time with the Eighty-Second,
I completed nineteen parachute jumps,
and for the first time in my life, I finally
accomplished something that was

important to me. But, just like my early school years, I still managed
to screw things up along the way. However, this time my academics
were not my downfall; my screwups were a result of what I like to refer
to as being "young, dumb, and full of Bud." And the Bud I'm referring
to is that good, old-fashioned Budweiser beer.

My first screwup occurred after a long evening of drinking. When I returned to my barracks, my friends and I decided to turn on the fire hose to douse the other guys sleeping in their bunks. At the time, we thought it was the funniest thing ever, but nobody was laughing the next day when we were ordered to report to the first sergeant. He was pissed as hell, but because I immediately confessed to my actions, I received a very light sentence. I was ordered to complete two weeks of kitchen police duty.

My second screwup occurred a few weeks later, and this time my punishment proved more severe. One evening, I was pulled over in a small North Carolina town by a local sheriff for speeding. When

the sheriff approached the driver side of my vehicle, he looked in and immediately noticed four cases of beer on the front passenger seat. Besides being the driver, I was intoxicated and one year shy of being the legal drinking age. What made matters worse was that, during the motor vehicle stop, I reached into my wallet and flashed a twenty-dollar bill in an attempt to bribe the sheriff. The local sheriff reacted by saying in the most Southern accent I had ever heard, "Son, I am going to pretend that I did not just hear or see what you just did." I was then arrested for drunk driving and spent the night in jail. The next day, I was ordered in front of the judge and was given the option of either paying a two-hundred-dollar fine, with a year's loss of driving

privileges, or being sentenced to three months with a chain gang. Well, I chose the first option, and I didn't drive for a year. During that time, I also completed copious amounts of KP duty and was busted down in rank from a private first class to a private. However, things could have been worse; I could have seriously injured someone or spent those three months with the chain gang. The craziest thing of all was that this occurred in 1960, decades before the strict drunk driving laws came into being. I definitely did not appreciate losing my license for a year. But, in hindsight, I realize that in some way, that local sheriff may have prevented a horrific accident or even my early death. Up until that point, I didn't think twice before getting behind the wheel after a night of drinking. This incident definitely changed my outlook of what could go wrong and the possible ramifications of drunk driving. One thing I knew was that I didn't want to go to jail again or be assigned to a chain gang. That alone was enough to keep me from driving, especially after drinking.

And you would think that after changing my drunk-driving ways, I would have curtailed my other bad habits. But, as always, I did things the hard way. I continued to drink heavily and partake in the occasional bar fight. In the end, it took one incident in the army to change my way of life. While completing a parachute jump, a good friend of mine,

Robert Foster, was killed. Apparently, Foster's main and reserve parachute did not open, and he fell to his death by what is referred to as a streamer fall.

Robert Foster was from New York, and he was a few years older than me. He was always the voice of reason when I was about to get into trouble, especially for fighting or drinking. Foster was the first friend I lost, and as a result of his death, I realized that I had to straighten out my life and change my ways. Not just for myself, but because Foster would have wanted me to do so. Foster was a good man, a great paratrooper, and, above all, a dear friend. His death changed my life in so many

Robert Foster

ways. It made me realize that life was very short, and that it could all end in one swift moment. His death was also a reminder of what my father had said to me just before he died. He said, "Joey, you have to take advantage of what life has to offer, and once you put your mind to it, you can accomplish anything." Until that time, the only thing I accomplished was barely graduating high school and making it into the army. That was quite an accomplishment, especially considering my past, but it wasn't enough. I knew that I was capable of doing more, and that is exactly what I did.

After the army, I returned to the Philadelphia area and attended a college preparatory school. Even though I already had a high school diploma, there was not a college in the country that would have accepted my past transcripts. So, for the second time in my life, I attended high school. But this time I made a valiant effort, and, after two years, I was accepted into an actual accredited college.

I attended Waynesburg College in Pennsylvania, with the intentions of becoming a schoolteacher. Although I was somewhat older than all the other students, during my freshman year I pledged and became a member of the prestigious Phi Sigma Kappa fraternity. For the next four years, I lived the life of a full-time college student and returned home during the summers to work as a lifeguard with the Ocean City Beach Patrol. In 1967, I actually graduated college, with a bachelor of arts in elementary education and a minor in psychology.

After college, I decided to put my teaching career on hold and did something that most college-educated army veterans don't do. I joined the US Marine Corps.

Chapter 8 · Becoming a Marine

Joe Walters · Dick Walters · Caroline Walters · Bill Walters

You would think that after overcoming a long struggle with academics, becoming a paratrooper with the Eighty-Second Airborne Division, a graduate of college, and a lieutenant with the Ocean City Beach Patrol, some would be satisfied with what they had accomplished. But, for some reason, I wanted the next journey of my life to begin in Vietnam.

My two brothers, Bill and Dick, were already Marines, so it was not a hard decision for me to keep the family tradition alive. Therefore, at the end of 1967, I joined the US Marine Corps and entered Officer Candidate School (OCS) at Quantico, Virginia.

OCS is the entry-level training for potential Marine Corps Officers, which is comparable to recruit training for enlisted Marines. I graduated from OCS after ten weeks of intense training and was commissioned as a second lieutenant. I was then sent to The Basic School (TBS) at Camp Barrett, Virginia, for six months of further training with other newly commissioned officers. After graduating from TBS, my next stop was Camp Pendleton, California, for one week of logistics and then Okinawa, Japan, for another week of training. At Okinawa, I was issued my jungle gear and was instructed in true Marine Corps fashion to begin adjusting to the hot weather. Specifically, the weather I would be living in for the next year of my life: the hot, putrid weather of Vietnam.

On my last night in Okinawa, I went into town and visited one of the local bars. I was on my fourth or fifth beer when I noticed several men staring at me in disbelief. I immediately recognized the men because they were in my group, but I knew that they were concerned because they were breaking protocol. Only sergeants and officers could move freely; the lower-rank enlisted men were confined to the base. I didn't want to cause any problems for the men or have them worry that I was going to say something to get them in trouble. I decided to leave the bar, but on my way out, I stopped at their table for a few words. When I approached the table, I asked, "How are you guys doing?" One of the Marine's answered, "OK, we are just having a few drinks." The other guys just sat there and nodded their heads in agreement. I didn't say anything for a few seconds and replied, "I don't remember who you are, and I won't remember tomorrow. It is important that you don't miss troop movement; if you do, they will throw you in the stockade." I wished them well and left the bar knowing that it would probably be the last good time those guys would have for a while.

Now, fast-forward a week. I am in Vietnam, lying in my hooch, and waiting for my next order. I was still embarrassed about the running incident, and my mind was racing with anxious thought. I still had not been in the field, and it was evident that my time was going to come very soon. I must have dozed off, because the next thing I heard was, "Lieutenant, wake up. Captain Pacello wants to see you and Sergeant Quinn."

I thanked the runner, got dressed, and walked outside, where I was introduced to Sergeant Quinn, who had been the acting platoon leader before I arrived. I had heard nothing but good things about his fighting abilities and decision-making skills. Sergeant Quinn said, "Lieutenant, I have been with the men for a long time now, and I will do whatever it takes to make this transition as easy as possible."

Jim Quinn

Sergeant James Quinn was from Chicago, Illinois, and he was very different from the average enlisted man. He was twenty-six years old and a graduate of Loyola College. He had originally wanted to become a Marine Officer, but his acceptance was refused because of a problem with his vision. The Marine Corps would later change the requirements, but by that point, he was already fighting in the war. Sergeant Quinn had arrived in Vietnam in January of 1967, and the men referred to him as either Corporal or Sergeant. I had heard that while out in the front lines, he and a few of the guys got to drinking, and of course one beer turned into many. Before you knew it, this strong Irish Catholic from Chicago began to sing "My Wild Irish Rose." The company commander was livid, and at the very next company formation, he was allegedly busted down to the rank of corporal. The following day, they left the front lines by truck, and all of the men felt really bad for him. They were all looking down at the floorboards, trying their best to avoid making eye contact with him. To ease the tension, Sergeant Quinn, now Corporal Quinn, reached into his backpack and pulled out a can of Black Label Beer. He then popped open the top, took a swig, and began to sing "My Wild Irish Rose." The rest is history. From what I was told, it was Captain Pacello's job to send the paperwork to battalion for his demotion, but I don't think it was ever sent. The only thing that I know was that Captain Pacello always referred to him as Sergeant, and it wasn't my job to uncover this mystery.

When we entered the briefing area, Captain Pacello looked at me and said, "Good, I can see that you have become acquainted with Sergeant Quinn. We are moving out after morning chow, and your platoon will be point. We are going to Liberty Bridge, and we need to be there as soon as possible." Liberty Bridge was located in the Quang Nam Province and was utilized to move soldiers and materials across the Song Thu Bon to An Hoa. The bridge was constantly under attack, and it was our job to make sure it was not destroyed. Captain Pacello continued, "I want you and Sergeant Quinn to study the map and make sure that you guys know where you're going." While Sergeant Quinn was making sure that the men had their C rations and had filled up their water canteens, I thoroughly looked over the map to ensure that we did not get lost. Captain Pacello then gently grabbed the radioman by his arm and said, "Lieutenant, this is Private Steele, and he goes every-where that you go." Captain Pacello then patted him on the back and continued, "This is one good Marine." Private Steele smiled and stared at the ground for several seconds. He raised his head, looked at Captain Pacello, and said, "Thank you, sir."

Thomas Steele was nineteen years old and from Colorado Springs, Colorado. He looked no more than fifteen, and he had been in Vietnam for only a couple of weeks before I arrived. He appeared very frail, and to break the ice, I mentioned that he needed to get some meat on his bones. Without hesitation, Private Steele turned to me and said, "Lieutenant Walters, I will be right by your side until we arrive at Liberty Bridge. We are leaving as soon as you're ready." He broke a small smile

Thomas Steele

and continued, "Lieutenant, you don't have to worry about me. My grandmother makes the best homemade cookies, and they will fatten me right up. When her package arrives, I will be glad to share some with you. Now let's get ready to go."

Chapter 9 · Liberty Bridge

We left An Hoa and started toward Liberty Bridge. As we were walking near one of the local villages, several shots were fired at us. The first shot zipped directly between Private Steele and me. I have no idea where the second or third shot landed, because by that time, I was already lying facedown in the dirt. I looked over at Private Steele and asked, "Is this what it feels like to be shot at?" He gave me a funny look and didn't reply. To this day, I don't know why I said it—maybe it was just plain nerves. It could also have been that it was my first day in the field, and my platoon was point. I also didn't expect to almost get shot just ten minutes outside of the base camp. In a way, it was a wake-up call for me: this was my official welcoming to Vietnam, and the enemy was just letting me know that they would always be watching.

While lying on the ground, Sergeant Quinn yelled, "What do you think we should do, Lieutenant—just keep moving?" I knew from training that when sniper fire is coming your way, it is best to ignore it and get out of the area as soon as possible. I also appreciated the fact that Sergeant Quinn tactfully suggested what we should do without trying to belittle me in front of the men. Everyone knew that I was now the platoon leader, but Sergeant Quinn was the guy who had been there for everyone through all of the hell. Technically, I outranked him, but it didn't take long for me to realize that if I wanted to stay alive and gain the men's confidence, I had to listen to his suggestions. Captain Pacello then radioed in and asked, "What is happening out there? What are you going to do, Lieutenant?" I replied, "Sir, we are receiving sniper fire, but we are going to keep on moving." "Good." That was all he said, but several seconds later, he was back on the radio. "Lieutenant Walters, don't shoot at those snipers! That is a friendly village over there." I replied, "Yes, sir." If that was a friendly village, I thought, I would hate to see a village that really didn't like us.

As we made our way toward Liberty Bridge, I couldn't help but think about my first day in the field with Mike Company. I was surprised that Captain Pacello had made my platoon point. I later found out that he usually liked to assign easy jobs to new lieutenants, so they could get used to being in charge while he was just close enough to help. However, in this case, he didn't have much of a choice, since the other two platoon commanders were also new to the company. I think that Captain Pacello realized that it was an adjustment for the men, especially since Sergeant Quinn was no longer their platoon commander. I surmised that if a situation did develop while en route to Liberty Bridge, the men would look to Sergeant Quinn for guidance. This didn't necessarily bother me, because I knew that he had paid his dues, and I still had a whole lot to learn.

We arrived at Liberty Bridge during the late-afternoon hours. Other than the earlier sniper fire we encountered, our travels went without incident. The area of Liberty Bridge was set up as a tiny base camp that consisted of several well-dug-in bunkers lined along the Song Thu Bon River. On each side of the river were also larger reinforced bunkers that were not dug into the ground. These bunkers were made mostly of sandbags, and they contained firing ports for machine-gun fire. The bridge itself was made of wood, and on each end it contained concertina wire that was pulled across the road at night to deter any foot or vehicle traffic.

Once we got set up, Captain Pacello approached me and advised that we would be spending a few days at the bridge, and we would be eventually moving out. Captain Pacello also told me that this would be a good time to get acquainted with the men, because we would probably not see too much combat at this location. That evening, I traveled from bunker to bunker and introduced myself to all the guys. I was amazed that most of these Marines were still kids and had not yet had the opportunity to experience life. The men were very respectful and displayed the utmost loyalty toward the Marine Corps. While speaking with the guys, I actually felt right at home. They did not hesitate to bust each other's balls every chance they got, and it reminded me of growing up with my five brothers. That evening I was especially impressed with two Marines in particular: a Mexican American named Rickey Almanza and an African American boxer named Michael Payne.

Rickey Almanza

Rickey Almanza had arrived in Vietnam in March of 1968, and it did not take long for the company to realize that he was a natural-born leader. Rickey was twenty years old, and Corporal Payne and he were the squad leaders of our platoon. Rickey was born in Moline, Illinois, and he had grown up close to the area referred to as Hero Street. This street was originally called Second Street, and fifty-seven men from this area served in the military during World War II and the Korean War. There is a monument dedicated to eight men, all of Mexican descent, who made the ultimate sacrifice. Five of these men are Joe Gomez, Peter Masias, Johnny Munos, Tony Pompa, and Claro Soliz. The two Sandoval families are also a legend in their own right, having sent seven men from one family and six men from the other. Three of their sons were killed in action and never returned home: Frank Sandoval, Joseph Sandoval, and William Sandoval. Although Rickey was not from Hero Street, I think he felt compelled to do his part for the Mexican community, and he seemed very proud to be a Marine.

Michael Payne

Michael Payne, in my eyes, was the poster child for the US Marine Corps. He had the typical boxer's build and looked like one of the drill instructors who was always on your ass at Officer Candidate School. He was an excellent squad leader, and you could tell the men really respected him. While speaking with Almanza and Payne, I asked them if they had any questions for me. They looked at each other, and I could tell they had something on their minds. Corporal Almanza then replied, "Sir, because you are the new platoon commander, the men are curious about you. It's not that they don't like you. I just don't think they trust your leadership abilities yet. Lieutenant, is there anything that I can tell them about you that might make them feel more secure?" I was really impressed with how much sincerity these two displayed toward their fellow Marines. I thought about it for a moment; I didn't know where to start, but I felt obligated to tell them everything about my past.

So I told them about my family and my growing up in Philadelphia. When I mentioned that I was in the army, Corporal Almanza immediately interrupted my story and said, "The army! That's great—now what am I supposed to tell the men?" We all laughed, and I reassured both of them that if they allowed me to continue, I would be able to explain further. Corporal Payne then looked at me and said, "Go on, Lieutenant." I continued, "I wasn't just in the army. I was a paratrooper with the Eighty-Second Airborne Division. I reached my two years of service and was held over an extra four months because of the Berlin Crisis. After the army, I attended Waynesburg College in Pennsylvania and worked summers as a lifeguard with the Ocean City Beach Patrol. After the Vietnam War began, I felt a strong obligation to serve my country. Therefore, I joined the US Marine Corps and was sent to Vietnam."

Corporal Almanza then replied, "Lieutenant, I will pass the word on to the men that you do have some military experience. I think this will make them feel a little better, because we have had a few platoon commanders but they were all—" Corporal Payne interrupted him before he could finish his sentence, though I had a good idea what Almanza was trying to say. "Sir, what Rickey is trying to say is that the men just want a good leader, like Sergeant Quinn, who is going to make good decisions and not get the men killed. I think the guys will also be happy to know that if they fall in the river and begin to drown, you can use your lifeguarding skills to jump in and save them." We all laughed, and I thanked them for their advice.

That evening, I learned a lot about the men: where they were from, how old they were, and that a Marine scout observer named Dirty Dan was one of the best combat fighters in all of Vietnam. Dan Hignight had grown up in several foster homes, and the Marine Corps was the only family he knew. It was known to all the men that Dirty Dan was very experienced with warfare, and that he was very loyal to Captain Pacello. A few months before I arrived, Dan had been involved with the

Dan Hignight

battle for Hue City. During this battle, 147 Marines were killed and 857 were injured. At the time, Dan was assigned to Lima Company Third Battalion/Fifth Marines as a scout observer and a tunnel rat when needed. One day, while attempting to clear a building, Dan came face to face with an NVA officer. With no time to react, the NVA officer pointed a pistol in his direction and shot him in the head. When Dan awoke, he was lying on the ground, and he had blood flowing from his ears and nose. Apparently, the bullet had deflected off of his helmet, and he was immediately knocked unconscious. It could be surmised that the NVA officer assumed he was dead, because otherwise he probably would have finished him off. A few weeks later, Dan was assigned to India Company, and his platoon was overrun by a large NVA force. It was a very dark night, and Dan knew that his only chance of survival was to play dead. As he lay perfectly still, he could hear several of them walking toward him, talking to each other like they were taking a stroll through the park. An NVA soldier bent down next to him and removed his wristwatch and wallet from his pocket. Dan never made a sound and lived to tell this story.

It was made very clear to me that evening that Dirty Dan was someone who I would never want to cross, and that I should keep him very close to me. When I asked one of the young Marines why they called him Dirty Dan, he simply replied, "Sir, that is a whole different story, and if you're here long enough, you will find out on your own." After speaking with the men, I made it my main priority the following morning to find this Marine named Dirty Dan.

When I awoke that morning, I left my foxhole and met up with Sergeant Quinn, who was eating chow with Private Steele. When I say chow, I am referring to our C rations, which were nothing more than prepared crap in a can. Sergeant Quinn received a radio call, and the Marine on the other end said, "I have the cream and sugar, if you have the coffee." Sergeant Quinn laughed and replied, "Dan, that sounds like a real good idea." Private Steele then turned to me and said, "That was Dirty Dan, and whenever he wants to come down for a visit, he gives Sergeant Quinn that same line about having the cream and sugar. I guess you can call it code for 'why don't you come down to hang out and shoot the breeze.'"

While we were sitting there eating our chow, a very tall Marine approached. Before he could say anything, Sergeant Quinn asked him if he had brought the cream and sugar. The Marine replied, "You're not getting any cream and sugar unless you have the coffee." They both laughed, and Sergeant Quinn turned to me and said, "Lieutenant Walters, this is Corporal Dan Hignight."

My first reaction when meeting Dan was that I could not believe this was the same guy all the men sat around and told stories about. The Dirty Dan I heard about was this John Wayne–type who wouldn't think twice about jumping down a tunnel to chase after the enemy or who would roam the jungle at night by himself. The Dan Hignight I met was very polite, and he seemed just like one of the guys. He had to be at least six foot six and was very skinny. However, while speaking with him, I noticed that he had a certain look in his eyes that said he was not one to mess with.

While Corporal Hignight and Sergeant Quinn were having their coffee, I started to eat my food. A young Vietnamese boy came up to us and asked, "My mother wants to know if you want her to make food for you? She will make the rice, if you will share your food." Before I could reply, Sergeant Quinn said, "Lieutenant, this is Lemonade Tony. He is a good boy, and he thinks that the Viet Cong are

Lemonade Tony · Jim Quinn

number ten." Lemonade Tony replied, "GI number one, VC number ten." I then told Tony that he could have my C rations, but he would have to taste the food in front of me when he brought it back. As the young boy walked away, I could see that Private Steele was confused, and I felt obligated to explain. I continued, "I heard that sometimes they

Rickey Almanza · Joe Walters · Jim Quinn · Michael Payne

will put little pieces of broken glass in your food, and before you know, you're shitting red." Private Steele laughed and replied, "Thank God, I don't have to worry about that with my grandmother's cookies."

A short time later, Lemonade Tony returned carrying a big pot of food. As he proceeded to take a few bites from the pot, I couldn't help noticing Private Steele staring him down like a vulture. After Private Steele gave me the thumbs-up signal that the food was all right, I told Lemonade Tony to come back later in the day, and we would give him more food. A few hours later, Lemonade Tony returned, but this time he was carrying a glass of lemonade. But what made this so unique was that the glass contained what appeared to be large chunks of ice. This was amazing because Lemonade Tony lived in a village that contained no running water or electricity, right next to Liberty Bridge. To this day, I don't know where or how Tony made the ice, but I can't deny the fact that his mother's lemonade was very refreshing.

The first five days at Liberty
Bridge, especially for the rest
of Mike Company, were a much-
needed break. When I joined
the company, the men had just
returned from the Arizona
Territory. In addition to the
terrain, this territory had been
given the name Arizona because
the Viet Cong fighters who fought
in the area were compared to
cowboys from the Wild West.

Joe Walters

These fighters were tough as hell, and unfortunately a lot of Marines
lost their lives in the Arizona Territory. When we arrived at the bridge,
Captain Pacello told me that our first couple of days would be "easy
work," and that we wouldn't be traveling too far from the bridge.

During the day, our duties consisted of searching the Vietnamese men
and women who traveled across the bridge. Most of these people were
carrying large bundles of chopped firewood and were traveling from
the mountain ranges toward Da Nang. I was astonished to see that they
carried the wood by stacking it on top of their bicycles or by utilizing
a small piece of bamboo to carry it across their shoulders. Either way,
it looked like very strenuous work, and you couldn't help but have the
utmost respect toward their work ethic. However, it was always in the
back of your mind that these hardworking people could also be the
same individuals trying to shoot you at night. Occasionally, you would
also hear the sound of gunfire coming from on top of the bridge. But
this wasn't the sound of Marines shooting at the enemy. Most of the
time, it was a piece of wood or a lily pad floating in the river. We had
direct orders to shoot anything in the water that was out of the ordinary
or any objects that resembled a possible Viet Cong soldier swimming
up in an attempt to blow up the bridge.

At night, we would deploy a small patrol on each side of the river
to set up a listening post or ambush site. Usually, we would not go
out very far, and we would return at first light. The ambush sites were
prearranged, and we would just sit there and wait for something to
happen. This duty was very uneventful, and for the first four days at
the bridge, we had no contact with the enemy. On day five, we left just
before dark, and it took about thirty minutes to reach our ambush site.
This site was on top of a hill, overlooking a small valley. That evening
a full moon enabled us to see very far into the distance. We had just
arrived when I observed approximately ten to fifteen individuals
walking directly toward our location. They were pretty far out,
so Sergeant Quinn and I decided to wait and see how close they would
come to our position. As they got closer, Sergeant Quinn whispered
to me, "Lieutenant, they're definitely the enemy, but I don't think we
should fire at them." I asked, "Why?" He replied, "They're well-armed,
and take a look at the last man. He is carrying a rocket on his back,
and he won't miss. We didn't have time to dig in yet, and that rocket
will blast us right off this hill." I wasn't sure what to do, because I knew

that Captain Pacello would have wanted us to try to nail them. I also knew that Captain Pacello had spoken very highly of Sergeant Quinn's decision-making and fighting ability. While I was debating what to do, the NVA suddenly changed their direction. They were still too far away for us to do any damage, so I decided to call in some artillery on their position. A few minutes later, fifteen rounds dropped in their general vicinity. The next morning, we checked the area but found no signs of wounded or dead NVA soldiers. When we arrived back at the bridge, Captain Pacello stopped me and said, "Your platoon will be spending the next ten days out in the field. You will be moving during the day, and at night you'll set up ambushes. Our orders haven't changed, and your main priority is to protect this bridge. You are going to be very far from here, so make sure the men have what they need."

That afternoon we left Liberty Bridge and arrived at our ambush site just before dark. This site contained two worn-out trails that intersected with each other, and you could tell that the Viet Cong often used them. In the middle of the night, a squad of NVA soldiers emerged from the trail, and we opened fire. The firing lasted only about a minute, but they didn't shoot back. The next morning, as we were searching the area, I heard one of the men yell, "There is a dead NVA soldier over here." Several of the men were standing there looking at the body, while others just kept their distance and looked the other way. I was curious to see what he looked like, and I had also hoped that he would have maps or other items on his person that would be helpful to the company. I slowly approached to where he was lying, and I took a really hard look. He appeared very peaceful and looked like he didn't have a care in the world. I guess you could say that it was his time to go, and he was now on his journey to the other side. Even though I should have been happy, I was filled with mixed emotions. I knew that we were just doing our job, but a man was dead. It wasn't like they were shooting at us, and we returned fire for our survival. We had opened up on them, in the middle of the night, with all of the firepower at our disposal. They didn't have time to react, and the only thing they could do was run like hell. This was the first enemy soldier who I came face to face with, and I felt responsible for his death. I don't know who actually fired the bullet that killed him, but it didn't really make a difference. I was in charge of the platoon, and I was the one who gave the men the signal to open fire. After this experience, my feeling about the enemy changed, and I accepted their death as being the only chance that my men had to survive. I guess it was like the old saying, "Kill or be killed."

I radioed to Captain Pacello and said, "We found a body. I think that he is an officer." He asked, "Do you have any proof that we can show the battalion?" I continued, "Yes, we have a weapon, maps, and other documents." He replied, "I will meet you at the riverbed by the village. Double-check the body and bring whatever else you find." We left our location and traveled to the riverbed to meet Captain Pacello. When we arrived, Captain Pacello carefully looked over the items we found and said, "Battalion wants proof of our confirmed kills, since there has been a problem with ascertaining the correct numbers. You guys did a good job last night, and I think these documents are going to be helpful for our operation. I have to get back now, but I'm going to be leaving a Kit Carson Scout with you. We have information that a weapon is hidden in that village over there, and he will help you guys find it."

A Kit Carson Scout in the lingo of the time meant "one who has returned." This was a program started by the Marine Corps that used former NVA and Viet Cong combatants, who had defected from the North Vietnamese, for intelligence purposes. Most of these scouts had left their villages because they suffered from malaria or other diseases that Vietnamese medical care could not treat. The scout interpreter who was assigned to our company seemed friendly. However, I think most of the men, including myself, did not trust him. I was careful not to speak tactics around him, and I just wanted to make sure that he was not a threat to the rest of the men.

After Captain Pacello left, we traveled into the village and questioned many of its inhabitants. Most of the villagers were reluctant to speak with us, but one woman agreed to give us information in return for a small amount of cash. While the interpreter spoke with the woman, he discreetly put some money underneath a large flowerpot. We stayed in the village for about an hour and left with the intention of returning for what she had to offer. When we returned, we found a weapon lying underneath some brush near a stream. The weapon was an AK-44 rifle, and it was so rusted that it probably wouldn't even have fired. The interpreter approached me and said, "If the Viet Cong figure out what she did, they will kill her. I don't think this old gun is worth her life, but at least it is out of their hands. The Viet Cong search these villages every night. If they find the money, the villagers will have some explaining to do. Most of these villagers are good people, but I think they have a general distrust of the Americans. I think they're just tired of war and want to live in peace."

For the next ten days, we spent the daylight hours searching for potential ambush sites, and at night we would travel back to set up. During this time, we were fortunate not to suffer any causality, and we had little contact with the enemy. On the last night, we walked across an open field on our way to a potential ambush site. Earlier in the day, we had checked out this site and found a trail that led into a wooded area. This area looked like an ideal place for the NVA to meet during the day and rest up in preparation for nightfall. That evening we were a good distance from the rest of Mike Company, and I felt very uncomfortable. I was concerned that if something did happen, we would be left to fend for ourselves. While we were traveling through the field, I thought I saw some movement. I signaled for the men to freeze in place, and I carefully scanned the area. At that moment, one of the men decided to have a drink of water and made a noise with his canteen. I wasn't sure if the enemy heard us, but I saw a lot of movement in the tree line just directly past the field. I turned to Private Steele and asked, "Did you see that?" He replied, "I saw something moving around over there." Corporal Almanza then crawled up and said, "Lieutenant, I know Charlie is over there, and this doesn't look good."

Joe Walters · Jim Quinn · Thomas Steele (Bottom)

I then turned to Sergeant Quinn and told him that we should move out and find a new ambush site. I also mentioned that once we got on our way, I planned on calling in artillery along the tree line. Sergeant Quinn replied, "Lieutenant, I couldn't agree with you more, and let's make sure that we don't miss." When we left the area, I could hear the artillery buzzing by our location, and I wondered if any of the enemy had been hit. Either way, this mystery would remain, because I never had the opportunity to find out just what happened. We were ordered to return to Liberty Bridge at first light.

The next morning, we returned to Liberty Bridge and joined up with the rest of Mike Company. It was nice to see all the guys again, and rumors were circulating that we would soon be moving out to our next mission. I was talking with Sergeant Quinn about our patrol from the previous evening when I observed Corporal Almanza and Corporal Payne interrogating Private Steele on where we were going to next. Sergeant Quinn said, "Lieutenant, you better get over there. They're squeezing Steele pretty hard. The radioman always knows what is going on with his platoon." As I approached them, Corporal Payne asked, "Lieutenant, do you have any idea where we're going? It seems like battalion gets their kicks off by keeping us in the dark." I looked at Payne and replied, "Battalion isn't keeping us in the dark. They're just keeping you and Corporal Almanza in the dark." We all laughed, and I continued, "As soon as I find out where we are going, you two will be the first to know." Corporal Almanza replied, "Well, here is our chance; Captain Pacello is walking up behind you." As I turned around, Captain Pacello said, "Lieutenant Walters, can I speak with you for a moment?" He continued, "I liked the way you used artillery last night to cover your movement." I told him what had happened, and he nodded in agreement and said, "We are leaving here tomorrow, so tell the men that they have a free day to get

Joe Walters

some rest. We will be having a briefing in the morning, and I'll go over the specifics then." I asked, "What do I tell the men about where we're going?" He replied, "Just tell them to get some rest, because we will be spending the next couple of weeks out in the field. I don't think it is a good idea to tell them where we're going yet, because our orders might change. Also, Lieutenant, being here at Liberty Bridge has been a good transition for you. You have had the opportunity to get some good field experience. However, I must warn you that it's going to be getting a lot worse from here on out."

The following morning, Captain Pacello held a briefing and advised us that we would be leaving Liberty Bridge. He stated that we would be flying by helicopter, and that we would be landing in a field next to a small village. Captain Pacello stressed the fact that the Viet Cong were going to be waiting for us, and we had to be ready.

As usual in the Marine Corps, we rushed the men to get ready, and then we sat around for a couple of hours waiting for the helicopters to land. I had just gotten off the radio with Captain Pacello when one of my men opened fire on a suspected NVA soldier who was walking in a rice paddy near our landing zone. Dirty Dan went to investigate, but before he did, he grabbed a few extra hand grenades and double-checked his weapon to ensure that it was loaded. He bent down to one knee and thoroughly looked over the area where the soldier had fallen. He then cautiously maneuvered across the rice paddy, and before you knew it, he was face to face with the enemy soldier. However, this wasn't an enemy soldier. It was an elderly Vietnamese farmer who was at the wrong place at the wrong time. Dan signaled to us that he was OK, and while he was walking with the farmer, the old man suddenly fell to the ground. Dan shouted, "Corpsman!" My corpsman, Eugene Whitbeck, ran out to help.

Eugene Whitbeck

Eugene "Doc" Whitbeck was twenty years old, and he was born and raised in Minnesota. He was also the only corpsman who I had ever known who volunteered for combat in Vietnam. Apparently, when he told his chief what he wanted to do, the navy sent him to get mentally evaluated. Doc Whitbeck wasn't your average corpsman. I had heard that during combat, he would not think twice about putting his body in front of an injured Marine. He was also known to pick up a rifle and fire at the enemy when needed. I had first met Doc at Liberty Bridge, where I had complimented him on how well he treated the men. I had overheard him reprimanding a few Marines on how they were not taking good care of their feet. He displayed a great concern toward their well-being, and I think the men felt a little more secure knowing that they had someone watching over them. The combat corpsman's philosophy was that the battle was not only with the enemy, but with time, proficiency, and above all "death" with whoever had the courage to lurk over the wounded soldiers.

I knew that something was wrong, because when Doc reached the elderly gentleman, he immediately began to work on him. After a short while, he walked up to me and said, "Lieutenant, I didn't even find a scratch on him. There was no blood; I think he died from a heart attack." At that moment, the helicopters began to land, and I thought, "This is not a good way to start a new mission." Captain Pacello then approached me and said, "Lieutenant, it's time to go and get the men ready to load up."

Chapter 10 · The Calm Before the Storm

We had just gotten off the ground when the helicopter I was riding
in started to receive sniper fire. Several of the rounds penetrated the
passenger compartment, but we were fortunate that the only thing hit
was Private Steele's backpack. When the helicopters landed, we moved
quickly toward the village. The helicopters were so loud that I was
actually relieved when they started to fly away. As we approached the
village, I was amazed at how quiet it was; the only sound we could hear
was a dog barking in the distance. My throat was dry, and I could
feel my heart throbbing through my chest. I had a bad feeling that
something tragic was about to happen, but before I knew it, Captain
Pacello was standing next to me, and he gave the order to move out.
As we entered the village, I said to Sergeant Quinn, "I don't get this.
Where in the hell are all the villagers? There is still food cooking in their
pots. Something is not right here." Captain Pacello then approached me
and said, "I think we scared them off. Corporal Almanza found a tunnel
over there; you're going to have to find a volunteer to go down there
and see if we can find any of the enemy." Before I could even give
Captain Pacello an answer, we both turned toward the tunnel, and all

you could see was Dirty Dan entering the hole with nothing but a pistol in his hand. Captain Pacello then shook his head and said, "Boy, does he have a set of balls. Go get some, Dan."

Dirty Dan found nothing in the tunnel, and Captain Pacello gave us the order to remain in the village until further notice. As I was walking around checking to see how the men were doing, I noticed one Marine who appeared to be talking to himself. This Marine was standing behind a small hooch, and he was staring me down. I thought that he had found something, so I walked over to speak with him. He immediately started to complain about the war, and it was difficult to make any sense of what he was saying. I wasn't sure what had ticked him off, but I became concerned when he approached me in a fighting stance. When he raised his arms, I immediately grabbed him and threw him to the ground with a judo hip throw. At the same time, Private Steele called my name and started to walk over toward us. When he saw that I had the Marine on the ground, he immediately went the other way. As I slowly let the guy up, I told him that he was lucky that I didn't have his ass court-martialed. As he walked away, he turned to me and said, "You never know when an accident might happen." I didn't say anything in return, but I was really pissed off about the entire situation. It was rare for an enlisted man, especially a private, to attempt to assault an officer. Also, this was during the time when there were rumors of officers getting shot in the back while out in the field. I knew this matter had to be addressed, but I wouldn't be able to do anything about it until we got back to An Hoa. At first, I even thought about mentioning this incident to Dirty Dan, but I knew that he would have probably beaten the living crap out of him or worse. Basically, I made it a point to avoid this guy at all costs, and the funny thing was that Private Steele never said anything about what he had witnessed. I didn't want this incident to be a distraction to the company, and I hoped that the situation would just work itself out in due time.

For the next couple of days, we stayed in the general vicinity of the village, with little contact with the enemy. We spent our days looking for potential ambush sites, and at night we would sit still, waiting for the enemy to show up. One afternoon, we stopped for a break, and I saw Corporal Almanza reading a newspaper. I asked, "What is the date?" He replied, "This is an old newspaper, but I think it is around the first of August." He then smiled and added, "Lieutenant, you have a long way to go." I laughed and said, "You got that right. I have been here for just over a month, and it seems like an eternity."

Since I had arrived with Mike Company, we hadn't had anybody killed in our platoon. In fact, nobody was even wounded. But our good luck was about to change. Corporal Almanza was right when he told me that the date was August 1, and the next day, I would learn firsthand about the horrors of war.

The morning of August 2 started off with a rumble for Mike Company. The point element was hit from the front, and they were fired on from the right and left flanks. Two Marines were hit, so Captain Pacello called in artillery, which briefly silenced the enemy. A short time later, we continued with our patrol, and we were ambushed by two separate NVA platoons. They opened up on us from two different positions, and we were caught directly in the crossfire. The battalion commander responded by laying a large barrage of 81 mm firepower, which silenced the enemy for only a short while. However, we continued to receive sporadic fire, while we remained persistent in trying to breach their front lines. Unfortunately, our attempts to break their line were unsuccessful, and we really got the daylights pounded out of us. While attempting to cross a field, one of the men from another platoon was struck while standing directly in front of me. This was the first Marine who I witnessed being wounded, and if he had not been standing in front of me, I would have been the one hit. I saw a tank that had been paralleling our position stop, so I picked up the wounded Marine and threw him over my shoulder. I didn't realize how heavy he was going to be, and I was glad when two other Marines ran over to help. We laid him down next to the tank and rolled him over onto his back. The Marine had been shot in the face, and it was obvious that he had suffered a fatal wound. I could hear enemy gunfire hitting the tank, and dirt was flying up all around us from the bullets striking the ground. I felt someone grab my shoulder; it was Corporal Almanza, who said, "Lieutenant, I didn't see where you went; I thought that I had lost you." I replied, "Almanza, I saw this guy get hit, and we had to get him some help." Corporal Almanza then looked at me with a concerned look on his face and said, "Lieutenant, I have a bad feeling about this place. Let's get the hell out of here." We set up a defensive position along a tree line and dug in, expecting a long evening of fighting. That night, naval gunships were used to keep a constant barrage of artillery on the enemy's position. It was a very clear, moonlit night, and we were constantly on guard because we suspected the NVA were going to try to overrun our position. Fortunately, they did not make any attempts to engage us, and by first light, the enemy had all disappeared.

This was a costly battle for Mike Company. There had been ten Marines killed while fighting for a very small piece of land. Worst of all, six of the guys had been killed by friendly fire. We also had fifteen Marines wounded, and their injuries were serious enough that some of the men would not be coming back to Mike Company.

We spent the next week conducting diligent patrols of the countryside, with minimal contact with the enemy. Our day and evening patrols received sporadic sniper fire, but we were fortunate enough that no one was wounded or killed. On August 4, Dirty Dan came upon a suspected NVA soldier who was burying one of his fellow comrades. The deceased soldier was probably killed a few days earlier and had been hidden until he could receive a proper burial. The NVA prisoner was cooperative, and I think most of the men respected the fact that he was only trying to bid farewell to a fellow soldier.

On the morning of August 8, Private Steele woke me up from a sound sleep. I had been asleep for about three hours, and it was the longest that I had slept since the An Hoa base camp. I had been sleeping so soundly, that when I woke up, I wasn't sure where I was. I actually thought I was back at home, but I was immediately knocked back to reality when Private Steele said, "Lieutenant, Captain Pacello wants to see you and Sergeant Quinn, and it seems very urgent."

When I entered the briefing area, Captain Pacello shot me a serious look and said, "We are in for some trouble. We are going toward Hill 310. You will be moving out with the weapons platoon, and your men will set up a listening post. The battalion will catch up with you during the night, and this will be the starting point for the attack. That is all you need to know for now. Good luck. Here are your coordinates; move out as soon as possible."

Hill 310 was a staging area that the NVA used to attack Da Nang, Da Nang City, and Marble Mountain. The NVA were loaded with firepower, and they took extreme joy in shooting at the American pilots who flew overhead. That afternoon we moved out and reached our objective without incident. Our orders were to set up a listening post, so we would be able to warn the rest of the company of any impending danger. Basically, we were bait, and our main purpose was to get the enemy to attack our position. However, if the enemy did attack, we would be in some serious trouble. We were approximately four clicks (four thousand meters) away from the rest of the battalion, and it is safe to say that we were out on our own. That evening, I instructed the men that we were on full alert, and that the enemy could attack our position at any time.

During the night, I went to check on the men, and I found one Marine sound asleep. I was so upset that I immediately pulled him up off the ground, punched him in the face, and pushed him partially down a small hill. Corporal Almanza and Corporal Payne then ran over, thinking we were under attack. When I told them what had happened,

Corporal Almanza said,
"Lieutenant, why don't you
go back to your position,
and we will take care of this
situation for you." When I got
back to my foxhole, Private
Steele asked, "Lieutenant,
what was the commotion over
there?" I answered, "I caught
one of the men sleeping, and
I lost my cool." Private Steele
continued, "Can't a guy get
court-martialed for that?"
I replied, "Yeah, he could."

Thomas Steele · Joe Walters

While sitting in the foxhole,
I thought about the situation and began to feel badly about what had
happened. At the time, I was so angry he had fallen asleep that I just
lost control. At Officer Candidate School, we were instructed to always
"lead by example." However, in this situation, my actions were very
unprofessional, and I definitely did not set a good example for the men.
So I decided to go back and speak with the Marine about what had
happened. When I approached him, he was sitting by himself, and I
could tell that he was upset. He asked, "Lieutenant, what are you going
to do? Am I in trouble?" I replied, "Do you realize that we are isolated
out here? Charlie could have easily snuck up here and threw in some
grenades. I know that you're a good Marine, and as far as I am
concerned, this problem is settled. I also shouldn't have hit you, and
I am sorry." The Marine cracked a partial smile and said, "Lieutenant,
I would rather take a punch on any given day than get court-martialed.
I'm sorry for putting the men in danger; it will not happen again."

When I got back to my foxhole, I began to hear the sound of artillery
in the distance. This meant that the battalion was on the move toward

our location, and they were firing at potential ambush sites along their route of travel. There was a tremendous roar put off from the artillery being fired, followed by the sound of the destruction it wrought when it landed. This was then followed by a long silence that would remain until the process would repeat itself. The battalion continued this barrage until they were a short distance from our location. At one point, Private Steele turned to me and said, "Sir, it sounds just like the Fourth of July." I replied, "Yeah, but without your grandmother's cookies." He said, "Speaking of cookies, that package still hasn't arrived." We both laughed, and I said, "Get Captain Pacello on the radio, and I will ask him if he brought your cookies." Steele gave me a serious look and said, "Lieutenant, please don't. That isn't even funny."

At first light, Captain Pacello called a meeting with his platoon leaders and sergeants. He had a certain look of intensity in his eyes, and he did not attempt to make any small talk. He advised, "We are going to take Hill 310. There will be three companies working with us to take the hill. They are Lima, Delta, and Bravo, from the Seventh Marines. They will be on the other side of the hill, and we may be supporting each other as blocking forces." Captain Pacello pointed to a smaller hill on the map and said, "We are going up that section first; it is called Objective Alpha. Lieutenant Walters, Second Platoon will be in the lead, so make sure the men are ready to go. It is already over ninety degrees, so ensure that the guys conserve their water." Captain Pacello started to walk away, but he turned around and yelled, "Wait a minute, we are also looking for a .51 caliber machine gun that has been a major burden for our pilots. Be careful; there are some hardcore VC up there, and they know we're coming."

Sergeant Quinn and I then held a brief meeting with our squad leaders and reminded them that the men would need to conserve their water. I also stressed that this mission was going to be the biggest challenge of our lives. While speaking with the men, I could see the fear in their eyes, and to be honest, I was just as scared.

While we were gearing up to move out, Private Steele approached me and said, "Lieutenant, it has really been an honor to be your radioman. I think of you as a big brother, and I'm glad that you're here. Can you do me one favor?" I replied, "Absolutely." He continued, "It is my job to be with you at all times; whatever happens up there, would you make sure that you don't leave me?" It was hard not to get emotional; I did think of Steele as a little brother. Because he was my radioman, he was technically right: it was his job to be with me at all times. But Private Steele looked like a young kid, and I felt I had to protect him at all costs. I said, "Steele, Captain Pacello was right when he said that you were an outstanding Marine. You are a good kid, and I really appreciate the fact that you never leave my side. We will get through this together."

At that moment, I remembered the advice that the war-weary lieutenant had given me at the An Hoa base camp. At the time, I didn't really comprehend what he was talking about, but after just a few days of battle, I now understood. I then looked Steele directly in the eyes and said, "Strength in numbers."

Chapter 11 · Hill 310

We started up 287, which was a small hill attached to 310. It was like a small spur, or thumb, but carrying all our gear made it an extreme challenge to keep moving. I was concerned about Private Steele keeping up, and when I turned around to ask if he was all right, he was in the process of taking extra ammunition from one of the men, who was having problems with the heat. We moved up the hill fairly quickly, and when we got near the top, we stopped to take a water break. Sergeant Quinn walked over to me and said, "Lieutenant, I found a trail over there, and I want to go check it out. It is probably nothing, but it is worth a try." I nodded my head in agreement and walked over to take a look. Sergeant Quinn had already selected a team to go with him. He pointed to a Marine named George Autobee and said, "You will be walking point; let's go."

As soon as they began down the trail, I heard the distinct sound of an AK-47 rifle. The next thing I heard was a violent thud and the sound of a man screaming as he hit the ground. Sergeant Quinn's instincts were correct; this trail led directly into an anti-aircraft bunker that included a tunnel complex. This area was heavily manned by NVA regulars, who were well equipped with automatic weapons and small arms. Sergeant Quinn and the rest of his team were now stranded, and there were rounds bouncing all around us. Unfortunately, we had to pull back and were forced to find a new way to get the team out of harm's way.

I had the rest of the platoon flank toward the left, where I thought it was possible to breach the line. While I was looking over the terrain, Captain Pacello came up and stood next to me. He proceeded to stand on the tip of his toes and was peeking over a small embankment. I said, "Captain, you better be careful, or you're going to get your ass shot." He subsequently ignored me and continued to look over the embankment like he was at a baseball game and was watching a play at the plate. He turned to me and shouted, "Lieutenant, get the rest of your men over here; those guys need help!"

We didn't know it at the time, but Dirty Dan had found a different trail that led to Sergeant Quinn and the rest of the stranded team. Just when he started to maneuver around a boulder, a Marine named Curtis Batten yelled, "Dan!" He threw Dan a grenade. Dan then pulled the pin and threw the grenade toward several hostile fighters. While Dan continued on his way, he decided to go around to the other side of the hill and approach the enemy from the rear. As soon as Dan was in the open, he was wounded by a hand grenade. Ignoring the pain of his injury and several incoming grenades, Dan was still able to pinpoint the enemy's position. Dan realized that the NVA who were throwing the grenades were not the main force, but a delaying force. He also knew that he would have to silence them before he could reach his good friend, Sergeant Quinn. Although the enemy continued with their barrage, Dan was able to maneuver behind them and deliver a grenade that put them all out of commission. Dan then continued his assault, using his shotgun to kill several NVA soldiers. Coming upon Private First Class Autobee, who was the first wounded Marine, Dan grabbed him and carried him to safety behind some cover. In the meantime, Sergeant Quinn was still out in the open, and he was having a hell of a shootout with the enemy. A short time later, a wounded Dirty Dan joined Sergeant Quinn, and together they fought for their lives.

At the same time, upon hearing the call for the corpsman, Doc Whitbeck ran in the direction where he was needed. Although observing that a Marine named Lance Corporal Tony Ayala was wounded and was on the ground between two opposing forces, he traveled across open terrain to administer first aid. When doing so, several hand grenades fell near him, and he maneuvered his body so that he would absorb all of the shrapnel. While Doc was moving Ayala to a safer location, Dirty Dan ran up and assisted. Dan told Doc that he needed to get information to the Captain, and he handed him an M-16 rifle. Doc grabbed the rifle, and without hesitation he began to fire at the enemy.

While Dirty Dan was trying to find Captain Pacello, he decided to charge the enemy gun pits. Armed with only a shotgun, he killed several NVA soldiers. When one of the soldiers attempted to crawl into a tunnel, Dan dove into a gun pit and began a fistfight with the man. While fighting with the soldier, he was surprised to hear, "Dan, don't kill him." When he looked up, he saw Captain Pacello and several platoon members standing around, watching the show.

While this action was going on, I saw several NVA soldiers attempting to flee from the hill. We found a blood trail and assumed that the NVA were trying to remove their injured and dead from the hill. My men started to follow the trail, but I immediately instructed them to halt. At this stage of the fighting, I didn't feel comfortable about the possibility of us getting separated from the rest of the company. The men were very stubborn, and in true Marine Corps fashion, they insisted that they could catch the bastards. I informed Captain Pacello of the situation, and he agreed that it was too risky. He also stressed the fact that the NVA could be trying to bait us into an ambush, especially because it would soon be nightfall.

I briefly glanced at my wristwatch, and I couldn't believe that it had been three hours since we first started up the hill. I took a good look around and saw several dead NVA soldiers and blood trails that led down the hill. Captain Pacello came to me and asked, "How are the men doing?" I replied, "Good, but a little shook up." He continued, "Lieutenant, let them know that they did a good job today, and that this is only the beginning."

After speaking with the captain, I noticed that several of the men were standing over a gun pit and yelling at the top of their lungs. When I walked closer, I came face to face with the enemy soldier who Dirty Dan had tangled with. I had no idea what he was saying, but it was obvious that he didn't like us. He was pointing his finger toward a large 12.7 mm anti-aircraft machine gun and gesturing toward himself, as if he was telling us that it was his. I asked one of my men, who spoke Vietnamese, what he was saying, and he replied, "Lieutenant, he is just letting us know that he hates our guts." The NVA soldier continued to disobey our orders, and it became apparent that he was not going to surrender in peace. He didn't even have a rifle or hand grenade, but it was obvious that he was going to get his point across whether we liked it or not. It was almost comical, but I think most of the men respected him for having the balls to defy our commands. However, his tirade ended when he attempted to grab one of our rifles and had to be physically restrained.

At first, most of the men looked at the prisoner in contempt, but slowly they started to have empathy toward him. Some of the men even offered to give him food, water, and cigarettes. Captain Pacello reminded us not to give him anything until the military interrogators were finished questioning him. He also said, "The fewer the people who interact with him, the easier it will be for us to extract vital information. Eventually, this guy could become a Kit Carson Scout, but I don't know about this one." I replied, "The only thing I know is that this guy is tough." Corporal Almanza asked, "Tougher than Dirty Dan?" I replied,

"No, but you can't help but respect his resiliency." Captain Pacello's forward air controller (FAC), Jim Blankenheim, chimed in and said, "They're all like this, Lieutenant, and there are many more where he came from. You haven't seen anything yet."

Captain Pacello called in a medevac helicopter and had Private First Class Autobee taken off the hill. Later in the day, because of mortar and enemy ground fire, the medevac helicopter was unable to land, and Lance Corporal Ayala had to be airlifted from inside a jungle penetrator transport basket. While he was being lifted off the ground, several NVA soldiers emerged from their spider holes and shot at the helicopter. Unfortunately, Tony Ayala was hit several more times and mortally wounded.

Our first day at Hill 310 was extremely hard for me, especially because it was the first time that my platoon had suffered casualties under my command. It was difficult not to second-guess my leadership abilities, and I wondered if there was anything else that I could have done differently. Basically, as soon as we made contact with the enemy, our mission became Objective Alpha. Once everything settled down, our next mission was to take Objective Bravo, which was the apex of Hill 310. That evening, I looked up toward the sky and scanned the 310 meters that made up the hill. I then turned to Private Steele and said, "This is going to be one hell of a climb, and you know those bastards are waiting for us." Steele didn't say anything at first and just shook his head in agreement. Then he looked at me and said, "Lieutenant, I have a very bad feeling about what we are going to find up there."

Just when I thought that things were settling down for the evening, the NVA fired mortars at the company. One corpsman and three Marines were seriously wounded. Captain Pacello countered the attack with a heavy barrage of artillery, and that was the last we heard from those cockroaches for several hours.

It had just gotten dark, and several of the men were eating their evening chow. Most of the men were hoping for a mail call, and when it didn't arrive, Private Steele started to complain again about his grandmother's cookies. I observed Corporal Almanza, who was checking on his men. He was particularly careful with the new guys, and he always ensured their gear was in order. I had just overheard Almanza reminding the men to ration their water intake when one of the Marines blurted out, "I have no water left." All of a sudden, Almanza jumped in this man's face and yelled, "I thought that I told you to conserve your water. It is hot as hell out here, and that water is your lifeline for survival." Almanza walked away and continued to eat his C rations. After about twenty minutes of giving the Marine time to think, he walked back over to him and put his hand on his shoulder. Almanza's look of frustration slowly disappeared, and a small smile crept across his face. He said, "You did a good job today. You have to remember that, besides our ammunition, you must also conserve your water. If not, you can pass out from heatstroke. Don't worry about it. Just make sure that it does not happen again." Almanza then took out his canteen and handed it to the young man. The Marine tried to tell him no, but Almanza nodded his head and said, "Take a drink, and, when you're finished, come over and eat with me."

That night, several of the men in my platoon opened up on "suspicious" noises they heard. I was concerned about them firing their weapons, because sometimes the NVA would throw rocks near your perimeter, hoping that you would give up your position. Captain Pacello called on the radio and asked, "What the hell is going on down there?" I replied, "The men think that they hear people moving around." He continued, "Tell the men to relax and not to fire unless they see some-thing." I told Sergeant Quinn about the radio message, and he informed the squad leaders that, if needed, they should use their hand grenades instead of their rifles. A short time later, approximately ten hand grenades were thrown into our perimeter, but no one was injured. In return, we threw a few grenades back; we had no further contact with the enemy until the next day.

On the morning of August 10, Captain Pacello and Dirty Dan approached me. The captain said, "Dan and I checked out what your men were shooting at last night. I guess they were right, because we found two dead NVA soldiers and several AK-47 rifles. More importantly, we found some documents that might make it easier for us to take the hill."

Colonel Seymour, who was the battalion commander, contacted Captain Pacello and informed him that it was now time for us to begin our attack on Objective Bravo. After witnessing firsthand all of the firepower that the NVA used during Objective Alpha, Captain Pacello decided we should move very slowly up the hill. When we started up the hill, we immediately received sniper fire from about five or six NVA soldiers. Two of our guys were hit, so Captain Pacello called in artillery on top of the enemy position. It appeared that several snipers were firing from inside a bunker and were not hit from the artillery. In response, Captain Pacello had a rocket fired into the opening of the bunker, which was followed by two separate explosions. Captain Pacello informed me that he was going to send my platoon up there on a reconnaissance mission. Before I could answer, Dirty Dan said, "Captain, why don't you let me and the other scout, Corporal Braya, go up there? These Marines make too much damn noise, and it will be easier and quieter for us to just sneak on up." Captain Pacello replied, "Dan, that sounds like a good idea, but be very careful."

When Dirty Dan and Braya got approximately thirty meters from the summit, they observed a sizeable force occupying the position. As they started to withdraw, the NVA opened up on them, and they just barely made it back to our location. Captain Pacello had Dan fire a M-79 round to pinpoint the exact location where he had seen the enemy. Once the round exploded, the entire hill erupted with automatic firepower. Captain Pacello smiled and said, "That was a huge mistake on their part. They just gave away their entire position. They're usually a little more disciplined, but this time they really screwed up."

At this point, Bravo Company decided they were going to attack the hill from the other side. When their assault began, one of the Marines was shot in the chest and died instantly. The Marine was almost at the top of the hill, and, due to the heavy enemy gunfire, the men from Bravo Company were unable to reach their fallen brother. They were forced to withdraw to a safe location, but they were not going to leave a man behind without putting up a fight. After several unsuccessful attempts, they deemed that it was too dangerous and decided to wait until the enemy gunfire halted.

Captain Pacello, after monitoring the radio and hearing what was going on with Bravo Company, called Colonel Seymour and requested air support for 310. Colonel Seymour ordered the companies to keep a safe distance from the target area until the bombing run was over. He also instructed us not to assault the hill and to remain in our position. Our plan was to mount an assault from the rear and respected flanks after the bombing was completed. Somehow, there was a major mix-up, and Bravo Company continued with a new assault about two hundred

Hill 310

Joe Walters (Left) · Dan Hignight (Center) · Frank Pacello (Right) · Hill 310

meters from the target area. As soon as they started to move, they received light enemy gunfire until they were about halfway to the target area. As they got closer to the enemy, there was less and less vegetation to use as cover. When they got to about fifty meters from target area, there was no cover left, and they were totally exposed to the enemy. The advancing Marines were completely taken by surprise, and all hell broke loose.

They found approximately thirty spider holes, connected by an elaborate tunnel system. The holes' small openings made it very difficult for the Marines to hit their targets. The NVA were able to pop out, fire a few rounds, and then take cover. Bravo Company was lured into a perfect ambush site, which was preplanned and had worked time and time again for the enemy. The NVA preferred to fight in close quarters, since this prevented the Marines from calling in artillery support. They would pick terrain that would leave the Marines unable to spread out and then concentrate all of their firepower into that area.

When the NVA opened up on Bravo Company, they hit them with a barrage of machine-gun and small arms fire. The NVA threw countless hand grenades that rained down shrapnel on top of the surprised men. The Marines fought back and were able to kill fourteen NVA soldiers. However, Bravo Company had eight Marines killed and eighteen wounded. A majority of the men were suffering from heat exhaustion, and they were down to only about sixty men. Colonel Seymour was livid about the mix-up, because basic tactics dictate never to make a frontal assault against an emplaced enemy when other options are available. Therefore, the colonel decided to have his battalion, the 3/5, attack the hill while the 1/7 would provide a blocking force. Basically, Colonel Seymour left the job of taking Hill 310 up to Captain Pacello and the rest of Mike Company.

August 11 was a busy day for the battalion. Mike Company continued searching Objective Alpha, which was where our company had captured the anti-aircraft gun. While sending patrols to probe Objective Bravo, we realized the NVA still had complete control of Hill 310. Colonel Seymour was anxious to bomb the hill, but he wanted to ensure that all the wounded Marines had been removed. The colonel had sent Lima Company to probe this area, but they were met with strong NVA resistance. Lima was fired on from six enemy positions, and one Marine was seriously wounded. The colonel subsequently ordered Lima to withdraw, and a new plan of attack would be initiated.

By the fourth day of the attack, August 12, we still hadn't taken our main objective. Colonel Seymour realized that it was pertinent to take the hill, and if we waited any longer, the NVA could have time to regroup. Since Lima Company was fairly certain that there were no wounded Marines on top of 310, Colonel Seymour decided to honor Captain Pacello's request to pound the hill with air strikes.

For the next three hours, I sat in awe and watched the most extraordinary display of firepower that any of us could ever have imagined. Napalm, high explosive bombs, and even CS gas were used to exterminate all living creatures that existed on the hill. After the bombings, Captain Pacello sent my platoon out to explore what was left of the mighty 310. The first thing that I noticed was that there was no vegetation left, and the trees had been burned down right to the stumps. Most importantly, we found a large stash of weapons, which included one M-60 machine gun, four M-16 rifles, one AK-47 rifle, one B-40 rocket launcher, four hundred AK-47 rounds, a Chinese assault rifle, and fifty-five hand grenades.

When we made it to the top of the hill, I felt like we had just climbed Mount Everest. Although Captain Pacello warned us that the battle was not over, we still managed to plant an American flag at the very peak. While the men stood around smiling and taking pictures, Captain Pacello was calling in mortar fire on an adjoining hill. A short time later, we were hit with machine-gun fire, and several Marines were wounded. After the Marines were pulled to safety, we once again pounded the area with a barrage of artillery. Private Steele then looked at me and asked, "Is this ever going

Jim Quinn · Joe Walters · Dan Hignight · Top of Hill 310

to end? I thought this was going to be like the game 'king of the mountain': once we reach the top, we win."

For the next two days, we continued our attack on the area surrounding the hill. On the evening of August 13, the whole valley was targeted by B-52 bombers. This was very eerie, because you couldn't hear the planes overhead, and the next thing you knew, the whole area was lit up like a fireball. The next day we were still receiving enemy gunfire, but it was becoming evident that the NVA were slowly retreating. That evening, I spoke with Captain Pacello, who gave me the best news that I had heard since my arrival in Vietnam. He had a look of relief on his face as he said, "Lieutenant, don't tell the men, but I think we're moving out tomorrow." As I was walking back to the rest of my platoon, I observed Corporal Almanza and Corporal Payne questioning Private Steele about the rumor of our possible departure from the hill. When I walked by, I looked at both of them and said, "Hey guys, Steele doesn't know anything, but I think the rumors are true. The captain doesn't want the rest of the men to know, so this has to remain between us. By the way, I told you that I would keep you in the loop, so stop harassing my radioman."

On the morning of August 15, we were informed that we would be leaving the hill before dark. In the meantime, a supply helicopter had dropped off beer, soda, and ice cream. This gift was a huge treat, and most of the men, including myself, overindulged like a bunch of schoolchildren. That evening, we returned to An Hoa thinking we were going to have a few days of rest and relaxation. Instead, our worst fears came true. After six days of nonstop fighting at Hill 310, Captain Pacello instructed us that we would be moving out the next morning to Goi Noi Island for a battalion-size operation.

Chapter 12 · All Alone

On the morning of August 16, we moved out from An Hoa and began the long walk toward Liberty Bridge. We were on a search-and-sweep operation, which meant that our battalion was trying to push, or sweep, the enemy into another awaiting battalion. We arrived at Liberty Bridge during the afternoon hours, and we were fortunate enough not to have

any contact with the enemy. However, we all knew that our next trip from the bridge to Goi Noi Island would probably not be as smooth.

When we first arrived at Goi Noi Island, the battalion had to make a river crossing with Mike Company in the rear guard position. The initial crossing went without incident; there was no way we could have known that the enemy allowed us to walk right by their location. The enemy was on the same side of the river as we were when we entered the water, and they waited until the rear guard of Mike Company was isolated from the rest of the men. Then the enemy began their attack.

Mike Company had successfully maneuvered across the river, with the exception of the Third Platoon, which was our rear guard. The Third Platoon was now trapped on the other side of the river, and the rest of the company was unable to help. At that point, Captain Pacello waded out into the middle of the river and began to yell commands toward the stranded Marines. The captain was by himself, and there was water splashing all around him from bullets hitting the river. I don't know how he didn't get shot, but I think that most of the NVA, and us, were in awe of this huge act of bravery. The captain was screaming, "Get up and get the hell out of there. Keep on moving." The stranded Marines were in complete confusion, and they did not react to his orders. Out of nowhere, Dirty Dan, armed with an M-60 machine gun, crossed the river and met up with the stranded Marines. Dan then rested the gun on top of a large rock and began to fire at the enemy. Captain Pacello was still having difficulty getting the besieged men to move, so, in total frustration, he yelled, "Keep on moving. I am calling in artillery, so you guys better get the hell out of here." Not sure if the captain would actually call in artillery, the men scurried across the river and rejoined the rest of the company. When the last man finally made it across the river, artillery rounds began to rain down on top of the enemy's position.

We were near the village of Phu Lac, which was our battalion's first objective, or Command Post #1. This village was known to be sympathetic to the Viet Cong and NVA soldiers. Mike Company was the lead element, and when we reached the village, we were welcomed with sniper fire. After securing this area, the battalion started toward Command Post #2, and once again we received small-arms resistance. After returning fire, we searched the area and found a dead NVA soldier, a Chinese assault machine gun, and several documents.

When our battalion arrived at Command Post #2, my platoon was sent out to conduct a patrol of the area. While walking along a tree line, we came across twelve enemy backpacks. This was peculiar, because the backpacks were positioned directly next to each other, and it appeared to be some type of NVA officer inspection. I heard a noise behind me, and when I turned around, I couldn't believe what I saw. There was an NVA soldier standing approximately ten feet in front of me. Our eyes locked, and initially neither one of us made a move. At the very same time, we both pulled up and pointed our rifles at each other as if we were in a Wild West showdown. The next thing I heard was a loud explosion, and I was immediately knocked to the ground. Apparently, one of the NVA soldiers had thrown a grenade, and by the time I realized what had happened, they were running across a rice paddy. When I stood up, Private Steele grabbed me and said, "Lieutenant, I think you have been hit." At that moment, I felt a burning sensation on my right arm, and I figured that the NVA soldier must have gotten a shot off before the grenade explosion. Doc Whitbeck then came up, and after a brief examination, he said, "Lieutenant, the good news is it's not a bullet." I asked, "What is the bad news, Doc?" He replied, "It's grenade shrapnel, and I am going to have to dig it out."

That evening, Doc Whitbeck removed the piece of shrapnel from my arm. I was relieved that I had not been shot, but at the same time, I wondered if I would have won the standoff with the NVA soldier. Either way, we were fortunate because the grenade had landed in a small ditch. I am almost certain that if it weren't for the ditch, we would both have been seriously wounded.

August 17 started off with a bang for Mike Company. It was a very hot day, and we were once again on the move. We were approximately twenty-five meters from a tree line when Sergeant Quinn observed several Vietnamese in uniform. We weren't sure if they were NVA soldiers or the good guys, so Sergeant Quinn got on the radio and asked, "Are there any Arvin soldiers in this area?" The command post replied, "No, definitely not." Sergeant Quinn opened up with his M-16 rifle, and at the same time, Dirty Dan, realizing the situation, opened up with a Thompson machine gun.

The enemy strength consisted of a reinforced rifle platoon with a large weapon section. We were not behind cover, and we were involved in a hell of a firefight with the enemy. At one point, a tank entered into the battle and assisted us by pounding the NVA. The next thing I saw was a Marine get hit, and without hesitation, Captain Pacello followed behind the tank and pulled the man to safety. During this heroic rescue, Captain Pacello was shot in the arm, and the bullet traveled up to his shoulder. Ignoring the pain, Captain Pacello climbed up on top of the tank and began to call in artillery on the enemy's position. Amazingly, he was able to remain on top of the tank in spite of the anti-tank missiles and mortar fire it was receiving. Finally, the tank commander looked up at Captain Pacello and said, "Get off my tank. You are causing us to draw fire."

As soon as there was a lull in the shooting, I crawled up to take a closer look. One of the other platoon commanders did the same thing, and we both ended up in the same mortar crater. As we were peering over a small mound of dirt, a figure jumped out and asked, "What the hell are you doing? I thought I told you guys to stay back there." When I realized it was Captain Pacello, I said, "Captain, you're bleeding real bad. Are you OK?" He replied, "I'm fine. Now get the hell back where you belong."

After the fighting stopped, we policed the area and found the bodies of six enemy soldiers. We also found a large quantity of weapons and other items that the NVA didn't have time to hide. Captain Pacello approached me and said, "I've been shot in the arm. I will stay here tonight; I don't want to leave knowing that the enemy is so close and could counterattack our position. By the way, you will be the acting company commander until we get a replacement. I recommended you to the colonel because of your prior experience with the Eighty-Second

Airborne, and you have also done a good job. You will also need to
replace your platoon sergeant. I recommend Corporal Almanza. He is a
good Marine, and he has been with the platoon for a while. Lieutenant,
just make sure that you take good care of my men."

Several minutes later, Sergeant Quinn limped up to me and said, "I
have some shrapnel in my leg, and I will be moving out tomorrow with
Captain Pacello. I just wanted to say good-bye, and I think that
Corporal Almanza is the right person to take my job. You have done
a good job, and I will see you soon." Sergeant Quinn shook my hand
and said, "Good luck, Lieutenant."

I was in complete shock when I walked back to where my platoon was
eating their evening chow. I had been in Vietnam for only two months,
and I now had to assume the role of the company commander. Captain
Pacello was one of the best leaders I ever met, and it was a privilege
to serve under his command. He had shown me that in order to be
an effective leader, you must not be afraid to put your own ass out
on the line. It was my Marine Corps dream to be in this position, but
after watching Captain Pacello deal with so many adverse situations,
I wondered if I would be able to handle this new challenge.

I also could not believe that Sergeant Quinn would not be with me
during my new endeavor. He was an outstanding NCO, and my job
would be even more difficult without him by my side. Even though
Sergeant Quinn was not an officer, he showed me how to do my job.
He never questioned any of my decisions in front of the men, and if
he had a suggestion, he would talk to me in private.

When I got back to my platoon, I sat down on the ground and thought
about my new responsibility. Private Steele then walked up to me and
said, "Lieutenant, I just heard the news, and I know you can handle this.
You're a good officer, and we all know you'll do a good job." I thanked
him for his words of encouragement and told him that my first mission
was to find out what happened to his grandmother's cookies. We both
laughed, and he said, "Please do; I don't know if I can wait any longer."

Corporal Almanza approached me and said, "Lieutenant, I heard that you were looking for me. But before you begin, I already know about Sergeant Quinn and Captain Pacello. It is definitely a small setback for our platoon, but we will be all right." Before I could reply, Almanza continued, "Lieutenant, I also heard that you were going to be our new company commander. Is that true?" I answered, "Yes, all the rumors are correct. I have one problem." Almanza asked, "What?" I replied, "I need to find a new platoon sergeant, and I was wondering if you have any suggestions?" Almanza looked at me and said, "I think Corporal Payne would do a good job. He is one tough Marine." I continued, "Almanza, I had you in mind. You are a good leader, and the men really respect you. You were also recommended by Captain Pacello and Sergeant Quinn." Corporal Almanza shook my hand and said, "Lieutenant, I will do my best, and I would also like to thank you for the opportunity."

The morning of August 18, I watched Captain Pacello and Sergeant Quinn leave in a medevac helicopter, and I never felt so alone. After they left, I was instructed that we would be staying in the area for the next couple of days. While I was mulling over the situation, Sergeant Major Bean approached me and asked, "Lieutenant Walters, I have nothing going on today, so do you mind if I spend some time in your company?" I had surmised that the colonel was concerned because a second lieutenant with two months' field experience was now going to be leading the men into potential hostile territory. I answered, "Yes, I'm glad that you're here, and I appreciate the help." Sergeant Major Bean then asked, "Lieutenant, do you know why you were picked to lead Mike Company?" Before I could reply, he continued, "Captain Pacello had recommended you because of your age and your prior military experience with the army. He also said that you were doing a good job and are very conscientious." I answered, "Thank you for saying that; it really means a lot." I wasn't sure if he was just being kind or was trying to reassure me that I was capable of doing the job. Either way, it didn't really matter, because I was just relieved that he was with us.

That afternoon, I had the opportunity to talk with Sergeant Major Bean about his life in the Marine Corps. During our conversation, a serious look came across his face, and he asked, "What do you think is the biggest regret that I have facing me right now?" I replied, "Sergeant Major, I don't know!" He then looked at me with sad eyes and blurted out, "I am fifty years old, and I have fought in World War II and Korea, and I have to leave the corps when I am fifty-five. I have been in the Marines since I was seventeen, and I don't know any other kind of life. The funny thing is that on the way over here, I was walking through some elephant grass and almost got shot. Corporal Hignight (Dirty Dan) and Corporal Bray jumped out at me, thinking that I was the enemy. Can you imagine that? I was laughing so hard at the expression on their faces, I was actually afraid that Hignight was going to shoot me anyway."

After we ate, I grabbed at my stomach and started to rub it. Sergeant Major Bean asked, "What's wrong?" I replied, "Sergeant Major, it is a little embarrassing, but I can't remember the last time I have actually gone to the bathroom." He laughed and said, "I always have to teach you young lieutenants how to survive out here." He stood up and said, "Follow me." Without saying a word, we walked over to one of the hooches, and he pointed to a large flowerpot and said, "That one is yours, and the other one is mine. Scoop out the dirt deep enough that your ass does not get dirty." There we were, the sergeant major and I, in the middle of a hostile area and doing our business in the most comfortable position you could ever imagine.

That night I had trouble sleeping. I couldn't help thinking about the Marines who were wounded or killed since I had arrived in Vietnam. We had been out on operations continually since I had arrived, and my biggest concern was that the company was losing all of its leaders. Captain Pacello and Sergeant Quinn were on their way back to the States, and the replacement sergeants and corporals had little or no combat experience. There were many new faces in the company, and my platoon still had only two squads. I was also well aware of the fact that I had not seen one man sent home after completing an actual tour of duty. However, I was very fortunate that Private Steele, Corporal Almanza, Corporal Payne, and Doc Whitbeck were still with the platoon. The next day was going to be my first operation as the acting company commander, and I felt a little more confident knowing that these men would be right there with me.

That morning, we moved to a new position near a river. Mike Company would be close to the river, and the other companies would swing around in a semicircle, with the battalion command post in the middle. I held a brief meeting with two platoon commanders, which turned out to be somewhat awkward. The platoon commanders had both arrived in Vietnam around the same time that I did, and we all knew that my position was only on a temporary basis. I passed on the information that I had received from the battalion and added, "Even though we are close to the river, I want to put out a listening post just in case the enemy does the unexpected." One of the platoon leaders replied, "I think this is a big waste of time, and the men won't like it." I continued, "Just do as I ask." My biggest worry was that the men would get complacent with the river toward their back, and I felt that with a listening post they would be more inclined to stay awake. After the meeting, the platoon leaders left, and we settled in for the evening.

The next morning, I was approached by the lieutenant who had questioned my order, and he said, "I'm sure glad we set up that listening post, because they tried to sneak right past our lines. We opened fire, but I'm not sure if we hit any of them. Either way, it was definitely a good idea."

That afternoon, we moved to a different section of the river, and the heat was unbearable. I heard some noise in the river, and I saw some of the officers and NCOs from the battalion command post in the water, enjoying the hot summer day. I radioed in and asked permission for my men to do the same, but my request was denied. I replied, "My men

don't think it is fair that only the brass are allowed in the water."
Whoever was on the line from battalion answered, "Good, a pissed-off
Marine is a better fighting machine." He laughed, and that was the
end of the conversation. The next thing I knew, a few of my men picked
up some rocks, and someone yelled, "Grenade!" By the time
the rocks hit water, the swimmers were scurrying toward dry ground
in a panic. I am not sure if any of them got hit, but it was definitely the
funniest thing I had ever seen. I knew this wasn't proper behavior for
an acting company commander, but I couldn't stop laughing. I just
hoped that nobody from the company command post caught on
to what had happened.

For the next two weeks, our company continued with several search-
and-sweep operations in the area of Goi Noi Island. During this time,
I was relieved of the acting company commander position by First
Lieutenant Barron. Lieutenant Barron was a good officer, and I was
actually happy to be back with Corporal Almanza and the rest of the
guys. Near the end of August, we had the opportunity to spend some
time at the Hill 55 base camp. This was no vacation, especially since
we were used to help secure the base perimeter. However, the men had
hot chow for the first time in several weeks, and we were able to finally
take a shower. Our first evening at the camp, we were given a lecture
about not allowing the local Vietnamese women to enter the lines in
order to have sex. The men were told, "If you let these girls into our
camp, you endanger everybody who is here. They will not only learn
the makeup of the base, they might actually blow themselves up and
kill Marines." The next morning, I got my ass chewed out because
there were rumors that the men had spent some quality time with the
Vietnamese women. I told the company commander that the rumor
was untrue, but I knew from the sheepish looks on the guys' faces
that the men had had some type of fun the night before.

By September 1, Mike Company was back on Goi Noi Island,
and the NVA activities were really heating up. My platoon was in the

rear guard, and we were also being kept in reserve for the company. During this time, I was beginning to feel paranoid, because every time we crossed a field or a rice paddy, we came in contact with the enemy. This day was no different. We humped for several hours and arrived close to our objective, when we came across an open field. This field was wide open and had no trees or brush for us to take cover behind. It also had thick vegetation at the end, which would be a perfect place for the enemy to wait for us. I didn't like the idea of crossing this area, and I said to Private Steele, "Here we go again." Private Steele replied, "Lieutenant, I don't like this at all."

The lead companies were almost at the tree line when the enemy opened fire. Over the radio, I could hear our company commander, Lieutenant Barron, asking another platoon leader, "What is the holdup? Let's get across the field as quickly as possible." Simultaneously, the tree line erupted with an extraordinary amount of firepower, and the battalion was stopped in its tracks. Several of the men were hit, which caused a great deal of confusion. The NVA appeared to be focusing on firing at the battalion command post, while at the same time just spraying the area with their AK-47 rounds. In return, the lead companies shot back at a very high rate, and it forced the enemy to keep their heads down.

I was surprised to see the battalion CP and one of the companies all bunched up in one section of the field. It seemed peculiar to see the headquarters section up front in the action while Mike Company was in the rear. If it hadn't been such a critical situation, I probably would have thought it was funny. My platoon was still waiting for orders when the enemy objective was targeted with air strikes. The jet planes had responded so quickly, and as they were wreaking havoc on the enemy, it was hard not to feel an overwhelming sense of satisfaction.

Just as I stood up and told the men to follow the lead platoon, the enemy hiding on our right flank fired on us. Every time we tried to move, they would just intensify their firepower. Lieutenant Barron yelled into the radio, "Hurry up and get your men into the tree lines." I replied, "Sir, we are directly in the line of fire. Could we use one of those tanks to get us out of here?" He replied, "Yes, but your troops must provide them protection and be in front of them in case they are fired on with rockets." I said to Private Steele, "Yeah, but who in the hell is going to provide us with protection?" I realized how dangerous it would be for a tank to enter this battle, but I guess I was just complaining like most Marines do, at times. There were several men wounded, and one NCO was killed during this firefight. Just before dark, a helicopter brought in supplies and removed the deceased Marine, along with the wounded men.

The company moved a short distance, and the terrain forced my platoon close together. It was like moving down a small dirt road covered with elephant grass of varying height. When I say grass, I don't mean the type that grows in your yard. This grass started at a foot high and in some areas was over the tops of our heads. Visibility was at a minimum; in most places we couldn't see twenty feet in front of us. It was starting to get dark, and the men dug in for the evening. This would be another sleepless night. I had several listening posts set up, but I felt that it would still be easy for the enemy to sneak up and throw in some grenades. My men were also very restless, and although I couldn't see them, I could hear their various movements. It was as if each individual noise was amplified and exaggerated ten times over. One man took a leak, which sounded like Niagara Falls. Another man was scratching his skin, and it sounded like sandpaper being rubbed on a piece of wood. As soon as I would shut my eyes, I would think that I heard the enemy trying to sneak up on our position. I guess it was fair to say that the NVA always kept us on our toes.

On the morning of September 3, it was so hot that I couldn't even eat. Instead, I took several sips of water just to rinse out my mouth. When I went to the morning briefing, we were informed that there was no clear intelligence on where the enemy was hiding. Basically, they could have been hiding anywhere, and it was our job to flush them out. India Company was going to push toward the objective, but not directly in front of it. Their plan was to walk on a slant, and the idea was to sweep toward the tree line. Our plan was to trap the NVA, who would attempt to evade the Marines by maneuvering around on the right side. We were ordered to move a short distance forward and then shift to the far right. Essentially, it was our job to protect the front and right flank because the enemy could try to maneuver around us.

I looked over and determined that our first objective was a tree line that was approximately the length of a football field away from us. We were about twenty-five yards from a dry rice paddy that led directly to our objective. We were all nervous because this area appeared to be an ideal spot for the enemy to set up an ambush. Therefore, I ordered the men to get down and remain in position until further notice. A short while later, my platoon stood up, and within seconds we were receiving sniper fire from our right flank. The squad I was with was then forced to dive behind a very small mound of dirt. The firing stopped, and the second we tried to move, copious amounts of bullets landed around the hill. At the same time, Private Steele handed me the radio and said that the company commander was on the line. Private Steele had a look of terror in his eyes, and before I even spoke on the radio, I reassured him that we would be all right. At that point, the company commander said, "You've got to keep on moving." Once again we attempted to move, but the firing just intensified. Corporal Almanza and Corporal Payne attempted to see where the firing was coming from, but, due to the elephant grass, they couldn't see anything. The CO then called again and said, "I thought I told you to get your men moving." I replied, "We are pinned down; we will move as soon as possible." There were several more bursts of fire, and during a short lull in the action, we moved as fast as we could to get away from the hot zone. When we stopped and got back on the ground, I could see India Company preparing to move across the rice paddy. Everything appeared to be normal, but I was definitely not prepared for what happened next.

Although we were the blocking force, I felt that we were very vulnerable for whatever the NVA wanted to throw our way. I also wasn't comfortable just sitting out in the middle of the elephant grass, waiting for the enemy to find us. We had already been sniped at from our right flank, and we couldn't see a damn thing around us. India Company started to move across the field, but they had to stop when their men walked right into our company's position. Private Steele turned to me and said, "Lieutenant, this doesn't look good." At that very moment, sniper shots could be heard all across the general area. The NVA then opened up from the front, with devastating effect. Bullets were striking all around us. Sniper fire was also coming from our right flank, from the same position that had fired on us before. Our only cover was the elephant grass, but there was nothing between the enemy and us that could stop a bullet. I just prayed that there wasn't a bullet meant for me or the other men in my platoon.

Mike Company was probably too far forward to begin with, and we may not have shifted over enough. We were still in high elephant grass, and I couldn't see a thing. It was tempting to just stand up and look, but I knew it was best just to remain in place. It was possible that the NVA actually opened up first from their spider holes, which in turn caused the tree line to erupt with automatic fire. There were spider holes all over the place, and they appeared to be connected to each other. Gunfire could be heard in various parts of the battlefield, and, for a short while, I actually thought that a much larger force surrounded us. The CO called on the radio and said, "Stay where you are until you hear from me again." I replied, "Sir?" But he was already off the radio.

Suddenly there was a lull in the fighting, and the only sounds I could hear were Marines shouting for the corpsmen. The shouting was also not from one particular area, but it seemed to be spread out all over the front line. Corporal Almanza crawled up to me and asked, "Lieutenant, what the hell is going on? Why aren't they getting any help? Are we going in?" I replied, "Somebody will be sent in. With all the chaos going on up there, I don't even know who is in trouble. The CO wants us to stay right here."

During the initial firefight, the company commander called me on the radio several times to make sure that we hadn't moved. I assumed this was because he was new to the company and didn't really know me or the other platoon commanders. Also, he couldn't see where we were and may not have even been aware of the sniper fire that was pounding us. All I knew was that I wasn't about to raise my head above the grass to see what was going on. However, I did look up when I saw the helicopters coming in, and I could hear the men yelling back and forth to each other about getting the wounded out. There was a lot of static on the radio, and it was difficult to understand what was happening. I asked Private Steele, "Can you tell what's going on?" He answered, "Yeah, the company commander is talking to Third Platoon, and they just mentioned about how their plans got messed up when the enemy opened up on them." Steele shook his head and said, "Those bastards had their own plan." Corporal Almanza then crawled up and whispered, "The men are in place. What do you think we'll do next?" I could still hear the wounded Marines screaming, and I didn't immediately answer him. Finally I replied, "India Company will have to attack the position. We can't stay here. The enemy is going to just pick us apart." Corporal Almanza asked, "Wouldn't it be better to just wait and see what they do?" I replied, "No, we have to get out of this area, even if it means moving forward and attacking them. The entire battalion is under attack right now, and we have to keep moving."

Private Steele then handed me the radio and said that the company commander was reaching out for me. The commander's voice was very tense, and he said, "Lieutenant Walters, don't move until further notice, but be ready to move at any minute. We are facing directly to the front, so it has been decided that we are going to make the assault. You will be next to Third Platoon and one squad over from First Platoon. You will still be on the right flank. Just make sure that your men cover to the front and to their right." I informed Corporal Almanza, and from the look on his face, I could tell he felt the same way I did. Neither one of us said anything, but we didn't have to. I had taken for granted that

India Company was going to initiate the attack. I knew that would have been the right thing to do, but now it was our job, and I wished there was another plan.

From the moment I was told that we would be starting the attack, it was hard not to panic. I could feel my hands shaking, and my back was starting to tighten up. There were many thoughts going through my mind, and I even rationalized that the attack was probably going to be called off. I then crawled over to one of my squads, and when I tried to talk, I found it difficult to speak. It kind of reminded me of my early school years, when we were forced to stand up in front of the class and talk about our summer vacation. I took a drink from my water canteen, and I became aware that some of the men probably saw my hand shaking. Private Steele looked at me and asked, "Are you all right, Lieutenant? I replied, "I am fine; I don't know what it is." Steele gave me a reassuring look and said, "We will be all right." The funny thing is that I was the one who was always telling Steele that things would be OK. Now, my radioman, who I looked after like a younger brother, was letting me know that he had my back. I thanked Steele, and I told him, "When we get out of this situation, I will definitely find out what happened to your grandmother's cookies." Steele laughed and said, "Lieutenant, I gave up on them a long time ago. I bet some guy in the mail room really enjoyed them."

Corporal Almanza then crawled up and asked, "Lieutenant, are we still making the attack?" I replied, "We can only wait and see." He left, and several minutes later, the company commander came across the radio and said, "We are moving out now. Have your men get on line and make sure they keep up with Third Platoon."

I didn't hear the order to attack until one of my men yelled, "They're moving." We jumped up and immediately attempted to maintain contact with the other platoon, but it was difficult to see where they were. We finally locked in with them, but the elephant grass once again forced us to lose contact. We were eventually able to rejoin the assault line, and I reminded the men to spread out but maintain contact. It was almost impossible, since the terrain at times forced us to bunch up and walk directly in front of each other. Because of the earlier attack by India Company, I had a good idea where the NVA were hiding. I was concerned that the enemy had dug in to either bunkers or spider holes that were well camouflaged and would provide them with excellent concealment.

It was hard to know exactly what was happening, and the rest of my platoon was only about eighty yards from the objective. I couldn't see the enemy, but at the time, we were being shot at from our right flank, and it seemed like the snipers were all over the place. As we continued to move forward, the height of the grass would vary, but most of the time it was at least chest high. After traveling through what appeared to be an endless area of elephant grass, we walked right into a rice paddy. Then the NVA opened up.

When the enemy opened fire, it reminded me of getting punched directly in the face. My platoon was surrounded by complete chaos, and we were trying to follow our orders, which were to keep moving. Around this time, Corporal Almanza saw that one of our men was seriously wounded. Ignoring the fact that he was exposing himself to an enormous amount of hostile fire, he deployed his men and encouraged them to deliver suppressive fire to the enemy. While attempting to cross an open field in order to reach the wounded Marine, Almanza was shot by an AK-47 round. Ignoring his painful wound, Almanza kept on trucking until he reached our wounded comrade. In true Marine Corps fashion, Almanza picked up the man and carried him to a relatively safe position. Realizing that the platoon was still in serious danger, Almanza continued to direct the men to keep moving, until he finally collapsed on the battlefield.

Corporal Almanza wasn't the only person injured while trying to save a fellow Marine. Doc Whitbeck ran across an open field, which exposed him to extreme enemy fire. Although he was in pain, Doc continued until he reached the wounded Marines. Dirty Dan was carrying a wounded man when he saw that Doc had blood all over his pants and running down his leg. Dan asked Doc, "Are you OK?" Doc replied, "Dan, I'm fine, so get the hell away from me." After Dan carried the wounded Marine back to the company command post, he immediately returned to help Doc. Dan started to pull Doc's pants down, thinking that he had been shot in the stomach, or worse. Doc yelled, "It's not my balls! I got shot right in the ass. Dan, I am all right; get back to the men."

During the height of the battle, my platoon was ordered to fall back. At the time, I didn't understand why, but earlier I had seen a tank heading in the direction of the Third Platoon. I just assumed that the company commander wanted us out of the kill zone before the tank started its barrage of fire. Several minutes later, I heard the tank firing as we moved away from the area. It was an uncomfortable feeling for me, since I had no idea what was happening to the rest of the company. We took cover behind a large dirt mound, and a short time later, the jets came in and dropped high explosive bombs. The enemy got the crap pounded out of them, and I just hoped that the fighting would stop for the evening.

A short time later, Doc Whitbeck approached me and said, "Lieutenant, I have been shot, and I am going to be leaving now." I shook his hand and replied, "Doc, you're a very good corpsman, and I thank you for everything that you have done for the men." As he walked away, the Doc turned around and said, "Good luck, Lieutenant." After he left, I remembered what several Marines had said about him while on Hill 310. Doc had just finished working on a wounded man, and one of our veterans said to a new guy, "If Doc ever gets shot, it will be directly in the bull's eye while trying to save one of us." It turned out that the veteran was right—that is exactly what happened.

After Doc left, I sat down and actually fell asleep. Next thing I knew, Private Steele handed me the radio, and we were ordered to move back and wait for further orders. When we moved back, we were in exactly the same position we had been twelve hours earlier. It was getting dark, so we spread out and waited for something to happen. Although I knew there were snipers in close proximity, I got the strong urge to brush my teeth. It was pretty quiet, so I knelt down and grabbed my toothbrush and went to work. Wouldn't you know it, but at that very moment, we were hit with sniper fire. Several of the rounds flew directly over my head, and I was forced to dive face-first onto the ground. When I looked up, Private Steele crawled up to me and asked, "Lieutenant, are you all right?" I replied, "I am fine. I was just trying to brush my teeth." Steele laughed and continued, "Where did you get a toothbrush from? Nobody brushes his teeth in the bush. No wonder they shot at you." Well, for some reason I carried a toothbrush, but that was the last time I brushed my teeth while in the field.

While the company was settling in for the evening, Dirty Dan had a different agenda. Dan went out on one of his famous solo missions to scout the area for possible spider holes, bunkers, and tunnels. As Dan was sneaking around, a very familiar voice caught his attention. When Dan crawled up, he found Corporal Almanza, who was still alive but seriously wounded. Dan picked up Almanza and carried him back to our location. At the time, we were in the process of setting up our nighttime defensive position. Private Steele approached me and said, "Lieutenant, it's Almanza. He has been shot, and it doesn't look good." When I went over to see what was going on, I saw Dirty Dan leaning over Almanza, and he was holding the corporal's hand. Dan was saying, "Hold on; don't give up. You're going to make it." To make matters worse, the sky opened up, and a heavy rain fell. It was now dark, and we were not going to be able to get a medevac helicopter to our location. Unfortunately, I had to pull Dan aside and inform him that Almanza was going to have to spend the night. Dan gave me a serious look and replied, "Lieutenant, he is not going to make it, but I am going to try to keep him awake." That evening, Corporal Almanza came to terms with the fact that he was not going to make it out of the battlefield. Prior to giving his last breath, Corporal Almanza said,

"Dan, don't forget about me." Dirty Dan, the toughest Marine in all of Vietnam, looked at his good friend, and, with a tear in his eye, replied, "I promise that I will never forget you."

On September 4, all of the NVA disappeared. Mike Company was pretty beaten up, and we spent the entire day searching the area for the enemy. We did not find anything of importance, and, amazingly, there was not one single round fired.

On the morning of September 5, we attempted to leave Goi Noi Island to return to the An Hoa base camp. It was raining really hard, and word was sent down from battalion that a typhoon was headed toward us. We moved out, walking as fast as we could, but once the ground became muddy, it was a struggle just to lift our legs. It felt more like a forced march, but we were not getting anywhere. Because of the slippery conditions, the men were falling down, and it seemed only to be getting worse. Our platoon was told to stop, and the company commander then held a meeting with the platoon commanders. We were huddled around in a circle, and the raindrops were stinging the side of my face. I was forced to keep my eyes closed, and the only thing I heard was when the company commander said, "We have to get to the river before it floods. I hope your men can swim."

As we approached Liberty Bridge, the wind was getting stronger, and the rain attacked us with even more ferocity. When we started walking, it felt as if we were moving in slow motion. It actually felt like we were trying to walk through quicksand. When I took a step and started to raise my rear leg, the mud would hold on to it while the front leg sunk even deeper. It was as though I was fighting an unseen force that had sided with the enemy, and it was another force that we would have to overcome. I was so frustrated that I told Private Steele, "This is crazy. Even if we get to the river, we are not going to be able to cross it until the storm is over." Steele replied, "Yeah, Charlie is smart. We are getting killed out here, and they're probably in some hooch getting laid." I laughed and said, "You know what, Steele, you're probably right."

While moving across the terrain, I was very busy making sure that the men stayed together and did not fall behind. Due to all of the activity, I had forgotten that Private Steele had been vomiting earlier in the day. He had managed to keep up with the rest of the platoon, but he was carrying much extra equipment besides his radio. I asked Steele, "I know you feel fine, but do you want me to take some of your extra gear? I can get some-one else to carry the radio for you." He replied, "No way, Lieutenant. I

Thomas Steele (Right)

feel a little tired, but no one is touching my radio. What would happen if they dropped it in the water? I also will feel naked without my extra rounds." Steele then held up two grenades and continued, "I also might need to throw these at the NVA."

That evening, we arrived at the river, and everybody's feet were pretty banged up. We stayed the night, and the next day we were flown back to An Hoa, which was a much-needed break. As soon as we arrived, Private Steele asked, "Lieutenant, do you mind if I go over and see if I have any mail, especially any packages?" I replied, "Absolutely." Steele returned a short time later, and I could tell by the look on his face that he had good news. He reached out with two cookies in his hand and said, "Sir, these are for you." I tried to tell him no, because I felt funny taking them from him, but he insisted. He sat down next to me, and I could tell that it was very important for me to eat them with him. Steele continued, "I decided not to open up my package with the rest of the platoon, because I did not have enough for all the men. But I want to share them with you because you're a good friend." I was really touched by his gesture, and at that point I realized that Steele reminded me of my younger brother John. My brother was around the same age as Steele, and in my opinion they were both too young for war. After I ate the cookies, I repeated to Steele what he had always claimed—that his grandmother made the best cookies.

While at the base, I saw two guys who I had met when I first arrived in Vietnam. They invited me back to their hooch for some beers, and that was exactly what I needed. As always, I was the last one up drinking, and when I left the hooch, I found Steele sitting on the ground and leaning against the building. I asked, "Steele, what the hell are you still doing here?" He replied, "Captain Pacello told me specifically that I go everywhere that you go. If you want to stay a little bit longer, I don't mind. It's kind of quiet out here, and when I get back to the men, I won't be able to sleep." I took him up on his offer and had a few more beers. The one thing I am sure of is that I don't remember the walk back to my hooch, but I know that Steele helped me get there.

The next afternoon, I was hung over. As I was walking through the chow line, I saw another Marine who I knew, and I said, "Hello." The Marine dropped his plate, which was full of food, and replied, "Jesus Christ, I thought that you were dead." We stood there looking at each other for several seconds, and I finally said, "Not yet." He answered, "I am really sorry. I must have gotten the wrong information." We sat and talked for a while, but neither one of us mentioned our previous conversation.

As we were leaving An Hoa on September 9, Corporal Payne came up to me and said, "Lieutenant, there is no one left. Out of our crew, it is only me and you, Dirty Dan, and Private Steele. My good friend Almanza is dead, and Captain Pacello, Sergeant Quinn, and Doc Whitbeck were all wounded. Worst of all, we're going back to Goi Noi Island, and we are heading straight for enemy territory." I didn't know what to say, but I nodded my head in agreement and said, "Payne, I am glad you are still here; we are definitely the last of the Mohicans."

Chapter 13 • September 11, 1968

On the morning of September 11, 1968, I woke up feeling uneasy,
angry, homesick, and above all, fed up with war. I was tired of the
fighting. I was tired of the heat. I was tired of the damn bugs, and I
was just plain old sick and tired of being in Vietnam. It was barely first
light, and it was already unbearably hot. All the men, including myself,
were miserable, which I guess wasn't that unusual for being on Goi Noi
Island. When I looked into the men's faces, and especially their eyes,
I felt that they didn't care anymore. This was just another day in
Vietnam, and the contact with the enemy was getting progressively
worse. The veterans just wondered when it was their time to die or be
carried off on a stretcher. The replacements didn't have a clue what was
happening, but they were well aware of the men who had either been
killed or wounded during the month of August. The main problem was
that we were all very tired. Although we had been at An Hoa for a few
days, most of the men, including myself, had trouble sleeping. One of
my major concerns was that the company was under strength, down to
approximately eighty men. Since my platoon had only about twenty
men left, we were forced to have two squads. Over the last six weeks,

Mike Company had lost many NCOs, and an outstanding company commander in Captain Pacello. I had just gone through two good platoon sergeants, Quinn and Almanza, and another one who was with us for only six days. I never found out what happened to him. My guess would be that he got reassigned out of the bush and into a safer job at the base camp. After fighting on September 3, I could tell that he was not very happy. He had been in the corps for a while, and I guess that he used his contacts to get himself out of dodge. Either way, I didn't blame him, because during his six days with Mike Company, we got the crap pounded out of us. And when I say crap, I mean crap. It was heavy fighting, followed by periods of downtime that consisted of little food, little water, and no sleep. The conditions were horrendous, and Private Steele summed it up best when he jokingly said, "This Goi Noi Island place kind of reminds me of Colorado. But Colorado doesn't have these bugs, this damn heat, this disgusting smell, and most importantly, there are no Viet Cong trying to kill you."

That morning, there was a company briefing, and we were told that our mission was just like every other mission we had been on for the past few weeks: find the enemy before they found us. It sounded like good logic, but there were no clear intelligence reports on where they were hiding. As always, we would be strolling into enemy domain while they awaited our arrival. During the briefing, the company commander, Lieutenant Barron, looked at me and said, "Your platoon is going to walk across the rice paddy and check out the tree line. If nothing happens, wait for the rest of the company to catch up, and First Platoon will take point. The platoons will flip-flop with each other, and if you're fired upon, shoot back, and the rest of the company will provide suppressive fire. We know that the NVA are out there, but where, is the main problem." I had a very uncomfortable feeling about this mission, but I also had the same feeling during the other missions when we were the lead platoon.

After the briefing, I went back to my platoon, and we shifted over so that we would be directly in front of our objective. Although I had not told the men of our role during the mission, they just assumed, like always, that we would be point. A short time later, the company commander came across the radio and asked, "Lieutenant Walters, are you ready to move out?" The company commander appeared to be in a hurry, as if it was important for us to get moving. Private Steele, who rarely showed any emotion, was trembling, and his body was shaking from side to side. No words were exchanged between us, but I knew that he did not want to cross the rice paddy. Private Steele had been with me twenty-four hours a day for the past three months, and his nervousness made me very uneasy. The company commander then came across the radio and said, "Let's go; the colonel wants us to move out right now." As we started to move forward, I reminded the squad leaders to remain spread out, just in case we got hit.

At the same time, unbeknownst to me, Dirty Dan was standing on a small hill, about five meters high, that overlooked the objectives. From his vantage point, he could see five NVA soldiers on the other side of the rice paddy. Dan then ran over and told the company commander about the enemy activity. Dan said, "Lieutenant Barron, there are some NVA over there. Look, they're right there." Lieutenant Barron replied, "I don't see any." Dan then grabbed the radio and attempted to contact Colonel Seymour in order to get air support along the tree line. Whoever was on the other end at the command post answered the radio and asked, "Who are you? Are you a company commander?" Dan replied, "No, I am Dirty Dan, and we need some air support out here." The unknown operator continued, "If you are not a company commander, you have to stay off the radio." Dan once again tried to tell Lieutenant Barron about what he had seen, but the CO answered, "I can't see any NVA, and it is too late anyway. Second Platoon has already started to cross the rice paddy."

When we entered the rice paddy, it was very quiet. Although Dirty Dan could see the enemy, we were unaware of their presence. From the distance, the area looked clear, but I still had a very uneasy feeling about what lay ahead. We were getting closer to the objective; I became aware that the last man had entered the rice paddy, and the point man was close to the tree line. At that very moment, a tremendous burst of firepower came from our direct front, and we all dove for cover. The only problem was that there was no cover; we were all in serious trouble. We were in an open field, approximately twenty-five meters from the enemy. We should have been able to see them, but they were in well-camouflaged, fortified bunkers.

What I will never forget isn't just the noise from the impact of the rounds as they struck my men—it was the noise the Marines made after they had been hit. Besides the usual cries for help, the men yelling for a corpsman, there was a distinct thud that the round made when it struck the body. The wounded Marine would then let out an unintentional noise as a boxer might do when he is hit with a tremendous body shot. Within seconds, the other squad started to take casualties. The grunts, groans, and cries for help sounded more distant and could be heard all over the battlefield. As the men were being hit, I could feel myself flinching with each round that made contact.

When I looked back at the squad, most of my men were either shot in the head or chest. From the time that we had been fired on to the time that I asked Private Steele for the radio, no more than thirty seconds had passed. My mind was racing, because I had never seen this type of carnage before, and it was safe to say that more than half of my platoon had been either wounded or killed. Private Steele had his head buried in his arms, and he didn't even look up when he handed me the radio. I keyed the radio and shouted, "Mike 6, this is Mike 2, and we need help!" I didn't get a response, and I was worried that we had lost radio contact. My main concern was that I did not know what the company commander would do. I also wasn't sure if he realized that we were close to losing the entire platoon. I was really upset that I had not received a response, and I once again yelled into the radio, "Help! We need help!" I tried to gather my thoughts, and I knew that I had to remain calm. I heard two shots come from the right side of the rice paddy, and a Marine yelled in agony. The enemy shot again, which was followed by another scream. I tried again on the radio. "We need help. Everybody's been shot. We can't move. If we do, they will hit us again." During this time, I could still hear the rounds striking my men. Finally, the company commander came on the radio, and he started to ask me questions about the situation. He asked, "How many men have been shot? How many have been wounded? Where are they firing from?" I answered, "Almost everyone has been shot. I can see four men who have been killed. Every time we move, somebody gets hit." The commander replied, "You can start returning fire now, and we will get you some help." I turned to Steele and shouted, "Who the hell is going to return fire? I think we are the only people left."

I still wasn't sure if the company commander understood the severity of the situation. I was also aware I had never seen a firefight inflict so many causalities in such a short time. I felt that I had to convince him that we needed help, and if he waited, we would all be dead. I was really frustrated, so I grabbed the handset and said, "Mike 6, we can't move without getting shot. They have a bead on us. I don't have any men left. It is only me and my radioman." I started to say something else, when several shots were fired in our direction. The next thing I felt was blood and brain matter as it coated the side of my face. When I looked to my left, I saw that Steele had been shot in the head; he was killed instantly. I got back on the radio and yelled, "They killed my radioman." At that moment, I saw another Marine, who was already wounded, get hit again. He rolled over toward my direction, and we made eye contact. I nodded my head that everything was going to be all right, but it was too late. The Marine then closed his eyes and died right there on the battlefield. I said something on the radio like "Oh my God" and dropped the handset as a bullet struck my knee. My leg rotated, and my kneecap felt as if it had exploded into many pieces. I picked up the handset and screamed, "I'm hit! I've been shot in the knee. Damn, I am going to lose my leg." The company commander replied, "Mike 2, we are coming! I need for you to remain calm and answer some questions for me. How many KIAs do you have? How many men are injured? Where are they shooting from?" I answered him the best I could, but I think I just repeated what I had said earlier. From the tone of his voice, I felt that he was going to do everything in his power to help us. It had a calming effect on me, but I felt deep down that I was either going to be killed or captured by the enemy.

As soon as I got off of the radio, I found myself trying to push my body into the ground. I was trying to dig a hole with my hands, but when I saw my fingernails were starting to bleed, I knew that I had to calm down. I could feel my heart pounding through my chest, and I thought, "Screw the enemy; I am going to die from a heart attack." I could still hear men yelling for a corpsman, and I even heard one Marine call out for his mother.

I then raised my head and took a good look at the ambush site. After several minutes, something changed in me. I was now somewhat calm, and my first thought was that I did not want to get shot again. I was lying face down and trying to push my body down into the dirt as low as possible. I was even trying to hide behind several blades of grass that were about six inches high. I wasn't sure if I was going to get out alive. I also knew that the NVA would not waste their energy carrying a wounded prisoner to safety. All I could think about was the Code of Conduct for American prisoners of war, which every US soldier memorizes. This code was drafted after the Korean War, and I had learned the six rules while at basic training for the army and at officer candidate school for the corps. Specifically, I thought about numbers two and three of the code, which read as follows:

"I will never surrender of my own free will. If in command, I will never surrender the members of my command while they still have the means to resist."

"If I am captured, I will continue to resist by all means available. I will make every effort to escape and aid others to escape. I will accept neither parole nor special favors from the enemy."

I knew what I had to do, and at that point, I devised a game plan; if I was unable to be rescued, I would fight until the very end. I slowly reached out, and I began to gather Private Steele's ammunition, hand grenades, and his rifle. I thought to myself, "What would happen if I ran out of bullets?" I thought about it for a moment, and I reached down and put a grenade into my pocket. I decided that I would save the grenade until the very end. If necessary, I would blow myself up and hope that I would take out as many of them as I could. But, in the meantime, all I could do was lie there helplessly on the battlefield. I could barely move, and I just hoped that if I were shot again, my death would be with little pain. At one point, I remember thinking, "They're never going to be able to get us out of this rice paddy. It's too dangerous. Who in their right mind would even be crazy enough to come out here after witnessing my entire platoon getting mowed down?"

Chapter 14 · The Rescue

When I came to, I said, "Shit, I can't fall asleep again." I guess because of the blood loss and overall shock, I was in and out of consciousness. I was in severe pain, and, to be quite honest, I was scared as hell. The gunfire was constant, and it was a reminder that I could be hit again at any time. I was lying on my stomach, playing dead, and every so often, I would lift my head from the dirt to look for the enemy. I didn't want to be taken by surprise if the NVA decided to move forward, but in this instance, they weren't budging from their fixed positions. And why would they? The NVA were smart fighters, and they knew that Marines don't leave their wounded behind and that a Marine, at all costs, will risk his own life to save another. In this instance, the other wounded men and I were simply bait that the NVA were using to draw the Marines into the rice paddy. As soon as a group of Marines got halfway across the rice paddy, the entire tree line would erupt with tremendous firepower. I was stuck directly in the middle of this equation, and it was obvious that the NVA had the upper hand. Basically, the NVA were holding all the cards, and all I could do was lie there and wait to be either rescued or killed.

I must have dozed off again and was awakened by the sound of footsteps approaching me from behind. I quickly turned around and saw several Marines running toward the kill zone. I shouted, "I'm all right! Get my men out first and come back for me later. I will be all right." I figured that I was probably going to die anyway, and I felt a strong obligation to get my men out first. This wasn't a heroic act on my part; I was just doing what any combat leader would do. If the ship is sinking, the boat captain never leaves until everyone else is off first. That was the way I was taught in officer candidate school, and that was the mentality I had witnessed firsthand in Captain Pacello.

Pfc. Bruce Jones

It was a proud feeling, seeing the Marines enter the kill zone for the rescue. It was one of the most heroic acts I had ever witnessed, and I just hoped that no one else would be wounded or killed. As the Marines began to carry out the wounded, the enemy firepower began to intensify. I saw one Marine in particular, Private First Class Bruce Jones, travel toward a rice paddy dike to help a wounded Marine. Jones was originally with the Third Battalion, Twenty-Seventh Marines. He was assigned to Mike Company in late August, and he was one good Marine. When Jones reached the dike, he reached down to grab one of the wounded. At that point, Jones was shot in the left arm; the bullet traveled through his arm, into his left lung, and then lodged directly into his spine. Another Marine ran up and pulled him behind the dike for protection. In one short moment, Jones went from rescue mode to being critically wounded. Private First Class Jones would survive, but he would never walk again.

Upon seeing Private First Class Jones and several other Marines either wounded or killed during the initial rescue attempt, the battalion devised a more strategic plan, dummy runs: jet planes would fly overhead and pretend to drop bombs on the enemy's position. It was hoped that the enemy would go deep down into their bunkers to avoid the bomb blast. A short time later, several jet planes started to fly overhead. I was unaware of the plan; I just assumed that the company knew that most of us were dead and decided to just blow up the whole place. Either way, I didn't really care, because I expected that I was going to die. I also didn't want any more Marines to be killed.

When the first wave of jet planes flew overhead, the enemy gunfire ceased, and the battlefield was taken over by a peculiar silence. However, the silence did not last long, and the sound of men screaming in agony filled the air. After realizing the jet planes didn't drop any bombs, I surmised that it was a dummy run, and I knew that the Marines had only a short time to enter the kill zone to get us out. The dummy run was broken up into three teams consisting of Marines from various squads. The Marines, just to name a few, were: 1st Lt. Howard Nielsen, SSgt. John MacDonald, Cpl. Mike Zang, Pfc. Ron Thayer, Pfc. Rich Reed, Pfc. Joe Freeman, Pfc. Mike Alden, Pfc. Jim Turnage, Pfc. Tom Wiseman, Pfc. Dennis Merryman, LCpl. Leslie Thompson, Pfc. James Hoyez, Pfc. Owen White Jr., and Pfc. David Johnston. All had volunteered for the rescue mission. They put their lives on the line, and when I first saw them enter the battlefield, I remembered thinking, "Ooh rah! Semper Fi!"

The next thing I heard was someone saying, "Lieutenant, we are going to get you out of here." I replied, "Don't take me. I thought I told you guys to take my men out first." A short time later, Private First Class Turnage and four other Marines reached me. By this point, I was semiconscious, but I remembered being rolled on top of a poncho and picked up off the ground. The men began to move very quickly, and the next thing I knew, I was dropped to the ground. I heard Jim Turnage say, "I've been shot in the shoulder, and some of the other guys got hit too." I yelled out, "Just leave me here! I don't want anyone else to get hurt." Fortunately for me, Jim Turnage disobeyed my order, and I was carried out of the rice paddy and into a safe zone.

LCpl. Leslie Thompson · Pfc. Richard Reed · Pfc. Joseph Freeman · Pfc. David Johnston

Pfc. Mike Alden

Pfc. James Hoyez

Pfc. Thomas Wiseman

Cpl Mike Zang

Pfc. Jim Turnage

Pfc. Ron Thayer

Unbeknownst to me, Pfc. James Hoyez and Pfc. Owen White Jr. made the ultimate sacrifice trying to save us: they were both killed during the rescue attempt. Pfc. Hoyez was from Albany, Oregon, and he had been in Vietnam for only three months before he was killed. Pfc. White was an African American Marine from Chicago, Illinois, and he had been in Vietnam for only four months before he was killed. Both James Hoyez and Owen White Jr. were still young kids and were courageous Marines. They were both killed trying to save me, a second lieutenant they barely knew.

While lying in the safe zone, I looked over and made eye contact with a sergeant from another platoon. The sergeant put his head down and said, "Lieutenant, I just couldn't go out into the rice paddy. You guys were slaughtered out there. I just couldn't do it. I'm sorry." Before I could reply, I was picked up and carried to another position to wait for the medevac helicopter. I then heard footsteps coming toward me. When I looked up, a bullet just barely grazed the side of my head. The footsteps were from another Marine, and I thought, "Damn, I've been shot, and I am probably not going to make it out of here. I think the enemy has my number today." A chaplain then came over and said, "I want to say a prayer for you." I replied, "You can say a prayer for me, but it is more important that you pray for my men." The chaplain started to say a prayer, and I looked up and grabbed his leg. I said, "If you are going to say a prayer, say it for the men, and you better not screw it up. Say it for the men; I am not going anywhere." The chaplain knelt down, said a prayer, and got out of there as quickly as possible.

Usually the H-34 helicopters were called in for medevac, but on this occasion, three CH-46 Sea Knights came in to get us out. As I was being carried toward the helicopter, Dirty Dan came to say good-bye. The last thing I remember saying to myself was, "Dirty Dan must be invincible." I was glad to see that he was all right.

The next thing I knew, I was in the helicopter. The copilot turned around to see what was happening, and he had an unforgettable look on his face. When I looked around the helicopter, all I could see were bodies stacked up on top of one another and blood splattered everywhere. As the helicopter was taking off, several rounds penetrated the metal, and some of the wounded were hit once again. When the helicopter abruptly turned, I saw Cpl. Mike Zang, Pfc. Ron Thayer, LCpl. Leslie Thompson, and several other Marines charging out into the smoke-filled rice paddy toward the enemy bunkers. It was scary but a great sight to see. I was concerned for their safety, but it suddenly dawned on me: I had been officially relieved of command. Someone else would have to lead the men now, and the war, for me, was now over. It was an emotional moment, and all I could do was scream out, "Go get those bastards!"

When the helicopter landed, we were at some type of mass triage area. A nurse came up to me and asked, "Lieutenant, how are you doing?" I replied, "I am all right." She took a brief glance at my leg and said, "We have a lot of Marines who need immediate care. Do you think you can hold off for a while?" I nodded my head and quietly said, "OK."

That is my last memory of being in Vietnam.

Dirty Dan Hignight "Entering the Abyss"

Chapter 15 · Where am I?

When my eyes opened, they were drawn to a large water spot on the ceiling. As my eyes were adjusting, I was overcome by a very anxious feeling. I thought, "Where am I?" At that moment, I felt tremendous pain in my left leg. When I looked underneath the bed covers, I remembered that I had been shot.

A young doctor approached my bed and pulled back my blanket to examine my leg. I asked, "Am I dead?" The doctor laughed and said, "Lieutenant, you have pulled through, and you're going to make it." I continued, "Am I still in Vietnam?" The doctor replied, "No, you're in Japan, at Camp Drake. You have been here for a couple of days." I asked, "Doc, what is today's date, and why don't I remember anything?" He replied, "Lieutenant, it is September 16, and you have been pumped with a large quantity of morphine and other drugs. You were in shock; it is not uncommon to black out and forget certain things."

While lying there, it was hard not to think about the horrors of September 11. I had lost my good friend and radioman Thomas Steele, and the majority of my platoon was either wounded or dead. I also wondered if things would have gone differently if Captain Pacello and Sergeant Quinn were still there, but I guess it really didn't matter. Rickey Almanza was dead, but I was relieved that Dirty Dan and Michael Payne had both survived that day of hell. Dirty Dan was the toughest Marine who I had ever met, and his acts of bravery had saved the lives of countless Marines during my time in Vietnam. Even though my life had been sparred, it dawned on me that I would never be the same person again. The person I was prior to war was gone, and the new person was just a shell of the old. The hardest thing was just thinking about how I would explain everything to my family — because at that moment, I never wanted to think or speak about Vietnam ever again.

The doctor returned a short time later, and I could tell by the look on his face that he did not have good news. The doctor did not beat around the bush, and he came right out and said, "I am not sure what we should do with your leg. If we amputate, you will lose it from the knee down. If we don't take it off, you may spend three years rehabilitating in a hospital. There is no guarantee that we can even save your leg. At best your knee will be fused together." I asked, "Doc, what would you do?" He took a long glance at my leg and finally replied, "Lieutenant, get a good night's sleep, and I will talk to you about it in the morning." As he walked out of the room, I remembered a Korean War veteran who would walk on the Ocean City boardwalk. He had a fused leg and would struggle just to walk a short distance. I didn't want to think about it all night or to be in pain for the rest of my life. So I made a quick decision. I quietly told the doctor, "Just take it off."

When I woke up, I was missing part of my leg, and I could hear a man screaming. The crying continued for a while. When the nurse came over to bathe him, I noticed that he was missing both of his legs and arms. Although this was a sorry sight to see, I would soon witness many other Marines whose bodies were in worse shape than mine. That evening, I was in severe pain, and I had a high fever. My bed was moved directly next to the nurses' station. I was covered with bags of ice in an attempt to lower my body temperature. I was hallucinating, and I could not stop thinking about the men from Mike Company who had been killed under my command. I thought to myself, "Did I do anything to get these guys killed? Was I a good leader? Would they still be alive if I wasn't their platoon commander? I should have been killed with my men; why am I still here? How the hell am I going to deal with this for the rest of my life?"

When I woke up the next morning, my fever had dropped, and I actually started to feel a little better. I knew the pain had to be excruciating, but I was pretty doped up on morphine and completely numb. A nurse came up to me and said, "Lieutenant, you look a lot better today. How do you feel?" I answered, "Nurse, I don't feel a thing. I guess that morphine really does work." I should have never opened up my big mouth because after that my morphine intake was decreased. I spent the next couple of days begging for the drug like I was an addict on the streets. The pain was tremendous, and at times, I actually wished that I were dead. However, these thoughts soon subsided when my mother and my brother Dick came to Camp Drake for a visit.

Before they even entered the room, I could hear my mother giving the nurses a hard time. My mother, the tough German woman from Philadelphia, ruled with an iron fist. We did not always see eye to eye, but I loved her dearly. She was a very demanding woman, to say the least. After my father died, I think a piece of her died with him. She was left with a prominent business, seven kids, and a very chaotic household. But, all things considered, she was a good mother; she always made sure that her children were provided with the best things life had to offer. We were spoiled, but nobody took advantage of her wealth. We were all just fortunate that, before my father died, he had the business savvy to set up a solid family trust that she could live on. She had been left with a considerable amount of money; therefore, she expected Camp Drake to have the amenities of a five-star hotel.

My brother Dick was first to enter the room. When he walked in, he had a look of fear on his face. I asked, "Dick, why is Mom yelling at the nurses? You guys just got here." I could see that Dick was a little less apprehensive now that I was joking around, and he replied, "You know Mom. She told the nurses that you should have your own room and that the food looks horrible." We both laughed, and he asked, "Joe, how are you?" I replied, "Dick, what the hell am I going to do with only one leg?" Dick then grabbed my arm and said, "Don't worry about that right now; everyone is just happy that you're still alive." I said, "Dick, you have no idea what I went through over there. I can't stop thinking about it. I don't know how I am ever going to get through this." My brother looked me in the eyes and softly said, "Joe, we will get through this together; just try to be strong for Mom's sake." It was painful to see my brother get upset, because he was one who never showed emotion. Dick was built like a barrel, and, a few years prior, he was the Marine Corps Heavyweight Judo Champion, a judo gold medalist at the 1965 Pan American Games, and he was now living in Japan and was training in hopes of making the US Olympic Judo Team. When Dick asked me to be strong for Mom, I understood what he was trying to say. My brother Bill was in the Marine Corps, and he had already served a tour in Vietnam. Bill planned on making a career in the corps, and he was slated to return for another tour in that hellhole. My mother's visit forced her to see the aftermath of what happens to a wounded Marine during war. Although I was pretty banged up, I'm sure it didn't take long for my mother and brother to realize that my injuries were incomparable to the other men on my floor.

When my mother entered the room, she sat down next to me and said, "Joe, your father would have been very proud of you. When we got the Western Union telegram, I thought that I was going to have a heart attack. The whole family is just so relieved that you are still alive." I answered, "Yeah, I'm still here, but my leg isn't." She then gave me a stern look and said, "You will get better; you have to stop feeling sorry for yourself. You did what you had to do, and now it is time to get on with the rest of your life."

OC WUO68 (P LLH571) GOVT RXT PD WUX PHILADELPHIA PENN OCT 4 1968 749PEDT

MRS CAROLYN WALTERS

    1139 WESLEY AVE OCEANCITY NJER

YOUR SON 9'30# 2-)534' 2ND LT USMC WAS ADMITTED TO THIS HOSPITAL

4 OCT 68 FOR TREATMENT OF AN AMPUTATIOM OF THE LEFT LEG ABOVE

THE NEE HIS CONDITION IS NEITHER SERIOUS NOR CRITICAL YOUR PRESENCE

IS NOT REQUIRED AT THIS TIME BUT HE MAY HAVE VISITORS YOU WILL

BE NOTIFIED OF ANY SIGNIFICANT CHANGE IN HIS CONDITION FOR FURTHER

INFORMATION YOU MAY CALL THE NAVAL HOSPITAL AT HO 5-4000 AREA CODE

215 MAIL MAY REACH HIM ADDRESSED AS NAVAL HOSPITAL WARD SOQ12 PHILA

PA 19145

    H P MAHIN CAPT MC USN COMMAMDING OFFICER US MAVAL HOSP PHILA PA.

850P EDT.

My mother's advice was very motivating, and after her visit, I vowed that I would take the steps to move on from the war and begin a physical training regimen. Don't get me wrong: the hospital had an outstanding rehabilitation program, but I knew that I had to do most of the work on my own. Eventually, I would be leaving the hospital, and when that time came, I did not want to depend on anyone but myself. I had lost a considerable amount of weight, and I was very weak. Prior to the war, I had studied judo, and I had a good understanding of the concepts of training the human body. However, I was now an amputee, and I was spending most of my days confined to a bed. When I did leave my bed, I had to be helped into a wheelchair, and this process was very embarrassing. The first goal I set for myself was to be able to get out of bed on my own. I figured that this was going to be a difficult task, because my upper body strength had totally diminished, and my right leg had not been used for some time. To accomplish my first goal, I began to incorporate some exercises while lying in bed.

A hospital orderly had given me a rubber ball, which I used to redevelop my hand and forearm strength. While lying in bed, I would grip and squeeze the ball for hours, while visualizing grabbing onto the bedrail to support my body for standing. Believe it or not, this exercise was very difficult. But after a few days, I could feel my forearms and grip begin to strengthen.

I did another exercise that consisted of lying completely flat on the bed and lifting my neck up and down. After completing several repetitions, I would contract my stomach muscles to the point where I thought I was going to vomit. I knew that a major component of getting out of bed depended on being able to sit up and then gear the rest of my energy toward the standing-up process.

Due to the fact that I was confined to my bed, it was very difficult to train my leg. One exercise I utilized consisted of pushing my foot as hard as I could off of the footboard of the bed. I would then switch and use only the ball of my foot, which strengthened my calf muscles. Within one week, I broke the footboard of my bed. After I broke the second and third board, I knew that I was ready to stand up on my own.

I decided that it was time to make my move. I began by sitting up, and I used the bedrail to swing my body toward the edge. I leaned over and grabbed on to a wheelchair and pulled it toward my bed. I was unable to reach down and lock the wheels, so I knew that my first attempt had to be successful. At that point, the Marine on the bed next to mine rolled over and said, "Hey, that is my wheelchair. What are you doing?" I answered, "I'm just borrowing it for a moment, so relax." He then shouted, "That is my chair, and you're going to get hurt. I need a nurse over here!" I looked at him and said, "Be quiet before I come over there, and then you'll really need a nurse." He laughed out loud and said, "Yeah right, come over here; you can't even get out of bed!" At that moment I snapped. I don't remember how I got out of bed, but I did. As I wheeled over to the shocked Marine, he sat up and said, "All right, Lieutenant, I was just kidding around. You officers are all the same. You can't do anything unless you get challenged to a fight." I replied, "Ooh rah."

As I wheeled out of the room, I was physically and mentally exhausted. However, I had successfully accomplished my first goal, and I knew that I was on the slow road to recovery. When I wheeled up to the nurses' station, a pretty young nurse looked at me in amazement and asked, "Lieutenant, how did you get out of bed?" I answered, "I just sat up and climbed out. It was no big deal." She continued, "Well, if it is so easy, would you mind helping me deliver the mail to the other patients who are on your ward?" I answered, "Absolutely, but would you mind if I start tomorrow? I am a little tired now, and I need to get some rest." She smiled and said, "Good job. Now, get back to your bed. I will meet you here first thing tomorrow morning."

The next morning, I began my shift as the floor mailman. I realize that this seems like a menial task, but it gave me the opportunity to get some exercise and meet the other wounded Marines on my ward. The exercise part was great; however, meeting the other men was a horror that would haunt me for years to come.

Most of the men were young kids whose injuries were far worse than mine. There were a lot of single- and double-amputees, who were missing both arms or both legs or, in some cases, one of each. I also saw a lot of guys who had been shot in the spine and were now paralyzed from either the neck or waist down. After seeing these sights, there wasn't one day when I didn't thank God for sparing my life.

Toward the end of October, I was told that I was ready to begin my next phase of rehabilitation, and that I would be going home to Philadelphia. Prior to leaving, I thanked my Marine neighbor who had angered me enough to get out of bed for the first time. I originally thought he was just being a jackass, but I had come to realize that he was just trying to push me toward the next step of my recovery. I told him, "You knew what you were doing the whole time. How did you know to fire me up like that?" He laughed and said, "When your brother came to visit, I heard him talking about judo and training for the Olympics. When I saw you doing those exercises in your bed, I figured that you were a judo expert too. That day, when you were trying to climb out of bed, I could see that you were very hesitant. When I failed to stop you, I knew that I had to distract you from thinking about it too much. When you flew out of that bed and started to wheel toward me, I thought you were going to kill me." We both laughed, and as I wheeled out of the room, he shouted, "Ooh rah!"

I arrived at the Philadelphia Naval Hospital in November of 1968. It was such a relief to be back on American soil and so close to most of my family, who lived about an hour away in Ocean City, New Jersey. I was assigned to the officers' ward, on the tenth floor of the hospital. This area was for the most critical patients, so I knew that my next goal was to get out as soon as possible. The doctors were very optimistic about my recovery. However, I was told that I would need several more surgeries before I would be able to be released. Most of my days were spent in the rehabilitation center, and besides working with the hospital staff, I continued with my own training. My rehabilitation was geared mostly toward being able to walk with a prosthetic leg. This meant that besides strengthening my right leg, I would also have to exercise my stump. These exercises consisted of moving my stump in all different directions in order to build up the muscles that had been weakened. I used a chair to practice standing up and sitting down. This was difficult at first, but, within a few weeks, I had to start wearing a twenty-five-pound vest because my strength was improving. I also did various calisthenics, which included push-ups, six-inch drills, and pull-ups.

Although my strength was gradually improving, I was down approximately sixty pounds from my ideal body weight. I was suffering from depression, and spending twenty-four hours a day in the hospital did not help. One evening, I decided to escape from my misery and took a taxicab to a local bar to get a sandwich and a beer. I was on crutches, so when I tried to open the bar door, I lost my balance and almost fell. When I finally made it through the door, all of the bar patrons were staring at me, and I heard one man ask, "Who the hell is that?" I didn't make eye contact with him, but when I sat down at the bar, I noticed that he was walking over toward my seat. He then asked, "What happened to your leg? Did you lose it killing babies in Vietnam?" I didn't reply, and when I stood up to leave, he slammed his beer down on top of the bar. He stood directly in front of me, so I could not leave. The bartender then got between us and said, "Hey, soldier boy, I think it is time that you get the hell out of here. I don't want any trouble here tonight." I nodded my head in agreement, and, as I made my way toward the door, I could feel the rage building up inside. I had heard that the veterans returning home were being mistreated, but I never expected this to happen in Philadelphia. I left peacefully, but I made a pact with myself that as soon as I regained my strength, I would return to finish this fight.

The next afternoon, the head nurse came into my room while I was doing some push-ups. She asked, "Lieutenant, are you OK? Did you fall out of your bed?" I answered, "No, I'm just doing some exercises." She gave me a funny look and asked, "How long have you been working out on your own? You are only supposed to do physical training with the hospital staff. What would happen if your stump opened back up?" I answered, "Your rehab training is slowing me down, and I am going to continue with my training until I get out of this hospital." The nurse smiled and said, "You Marines are all the same. I don't know when you're going to get out of here. But the one thing I'm sure of is that you do not belong in this room." That afternoon, I was moved to a room that was away from the nurses' station, which meant that my second goal had been accomplished.

The following week, I went back to my old room because I heard that a Marine named Lewis Puller had just arrived. Lewis Puller was not just an ordinary Marine. He was the son of the legendary Marine Corps general Chesty Puller. Chesty Puller had fought in five wars, where he accumulated fourteen personal decorations and five Navy Crosses. The general had survived countless battles and fought in wars that most people never even heard of. He was a Marine Corps hero, and now he was forced to witness his own son deal with the aftermath of war. Lewis Puller had both of his legs amputated, and both of his hands were severely damaged. I could tell that he was in a lot of pain, so I did not visit with him too long. After my visit, I said a prayer for him, and I felt honored to have had the opportunity to meet part of a Marine Corps legacy.

During this time, the main thing keeping me going was that my family was spending a considerable amount of time at the hospital. Their presence was actually a major motivating factor in my drive toward leaving the hospital for good. My brother John and I were very close. Even though he was the youngest member of our family, the bond we shared was very strong. John had started doing judo at age twelve, and, within a few years, he was able to beat most grown men. He spent most of his teenage years training in judo schools and competing in tournaments all across the United States. During this time, my brother Dick was at the height of his judo career, and together they made one hell of a team. The amazing thing was that John displayed the talent and natural ability to become one of the greatest judo players in the world. Some would argue that he had the potential to become even better than our brother Dick. However, John had nothing to prove, and by his early twenties, he had enough of fighting. John was a free spirit who enjoyed life, and he had lost his drive to conquer the judo world. John continued to train, but he would never compete again. We all knew that Dick wasn't happy about this situation, but there was nothing he could do. Judo was Dick's life, but John had different plans for his future.

When John visited me in the hospital for the first time, it was a very traumatic experience. John had reminded me so much of my radioman and good friend, Private Steele, that the memory of his death would not leave my mind. Private Steele had been killed under my command, and I felt responsible for his death. Fortunately, my brother John, due to a shoulder injury he sustained while doing judo, was unable to pass the physical to fight in Vietnam. This took a huge burden off my back, knowing that my youngest and dearest brother would now be safe from the horrors that had taken Private Steele's life.

My three older brothers—Raymond, Charlie, and Billy—also visited me. Raymond was the oldest, and he was a pipefitter for the Philadelphia plumber's union. Raymond had left the house when I was a kid, but we always remained close. Charlie was also in the union, and he was now living in the Philadelphia area. Billy was also in the Marine Corps, and he had just returned from a tour in Vietnam. I looked up to him because he was not just my big brother, he also was a good Marine. Billy was very intelligent and was using his brains to rise right up through the ranks in the corps.

My sister Caroline (Butchie) was married with a family. However, she devoted most of her time toward my recovery. Butchie was a tiny but strong woman, who was devoted to the Catholic Church. She was also the glue that had held our family together after my father passed away. A few weeks later, I was released from the hospital, and I had to return

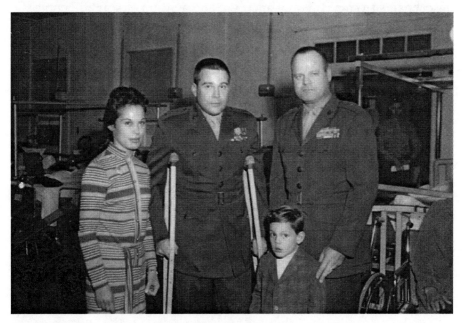

Caroline (Butchie) Ford · Joe Walters · General T. Olsen · Nephew Raymond Ford

every day for rehabilitation. I was unable to drive, and in a true testament to her character, Butchie woke up at four o'clock every morning and drove me from Ocean City to Philadelphia. Butchie would patiently wait for my training to end, and then she would drive the hour-long ride back to our home. Butchie already had two children, and, during this time, she was pregnant with her third. Butchie and her husband, Bob Ford,

put their own family aside for my sake. Without their assistance, I don't know what I would have done.

The term family often refers to parents and their children, relatives, descendants from a common ancestor, and a group of similar people. In this case, my family was all of the above, especially the part about a group of similar people. My family had pulled together at my time of need, and they all possessed the same similar goal, which was my recovery. Without my mother, my brothers Raymond, Billy, Dick, Charlie, and John, Butchie, and my brother-in-law Bob, I would not have been able to get through my transition from the battlefield of Vietnam to everyday civilian life. I guess you could say that this was just another example of strength in numbers.

Chapter 16 • Jersey Shore:
Spring and Summer of 1969

As I walked through the door of Gregory's Bar, I saw my brother Dick sitting at the bar. Gregory's was located in Somers Point, New Jersey, which was situated directly next to Ocean City. Ocean City was a wonderful place to live, but it was a dry town. To a single man in his twenties, this was a major problem, because there was no place to purchase or drink alcohol. Therefore, I spent most of my nights in Somers Point. That evening, there were plenty of seats open, but for some reason some guy was sitting right next to my brother. When Dick saw me come in, he pointed to two open seats and said, "We'll sit there." He looked angry, and when I asked what the problem was, he mumbled, "Sometimes, I just want to be left alone."

By this time, my brother Dick was well known in the South Jersey area. He was a Pan American champion in judo, and he was now training for the 1972 Olympic Games. You could tell by looking at him that he was tough as nails, and because of that, people often started fights with him for no reason. While we were sitting there enjoying our beer, that same guy walked over and tried to squeeze between our seats. Dick then put his hand out to stop him and quietly said, "My brother and I are just trying to relax. Why don't you just move down to the other end of the bar? I don't want any problems." The guy replied, "I'm a Golden Gloves boxer, and I'll knock you out." My brother didn't even react to his comments; he just sat there, staring straight ahead at his beer. I looked at the guy and said, "I don't think you want to do this. It is probably in your best interest to just walk away." The guy continued, "I'm not going anywhere, and I will kick your ass too." Dick was staring straight ahead, but out of the corner of his eye, he noticed that the guy was starting to raise his fist. Without leaving his bar stool, Dick backhanded the guy with a closed fist, and he was immediately knocked out. As the guy was lying on the ground, Dick turned to me with a concerned look on his face and said, "Joe, I think I killed him." The guy wasn't moving, and for a moment, I actually thought he was dead. The bartender then walked over, and by this time the guy was emerging out of unconsciousness. As they were dragging the poor sap out the door, he asked, "What happened?" One of the bar help quickly answered, "Tonight, you picked the wrong guy to mess with."

Dick ordered another beer, and we both sat there not saying a word about what had happened. A short time later, Dick said, "I shouldn't have hit that guy, but he kept on pushing me. I know you don't like violence, especially after everything you have been through. I'm sorry." I answered, "It's all right; he definitely had it coming. Next time, just put him in an arm bar or choke him out. He hit his head pretty hard on the ground and could have been killed." Dick smiled and said, "You're right. By the way, don't drink too much; tomorrow, we have some training to do."

After I was discharged from the hospital, I went to live with my mother at Twelfth and Wesley in Ocean City. Our house had a large detached garage that Dick turned into a gym. We had one of the first Olympic weight sets in the area, and the floor of the garage had been covered with mats for judo. Although I was commuting to Philadelphia every day for rehabilitation, most of my training was conducted in this converted torture den. I was lifting weights on a daily basis, and I started doing judo for the first time since before the war. When I was in the hospital, I had spoken with some older veterans who had become amputees during World War II and the Korean War. Their main complaint was that they were suffering from chronic back pain, and most of them were developing arthritis in the area of their stumps. I figured that doing judo would help develop my physical strength and also keep my mind distracted from the painful memories that would not leave my head. I also wanted to be able to defend myself if a situation did arise, especially if I had another encounter like the one I had in that Philadelphia bar. Because of the war, I just wanted to live the rest of my life in peace. However, the thought of beating the hell out of that guy was a strong motivating force.

Besides working out in the garage, I started to train with Dick at a judo school in Philadelphia. When Dick had won the Marine Corps judo championship, he had met Takahiko Ishikawa, who was the referee of his final match. Ishikawa was a two-time All-Japan Judo Champion, and he was now training students at his dojo in Philadelphia. Ishikawa had fought with Japan during World War II, where he was captured and taken prisoner by the Soviet army. During his captivity, Ishikawa was forced into slave labor, but he was fortunate to have survived the war. Ishikawa eventually immigrated to the United States, where he and his wife raised their family. Ishikawa was an eighth-degree black belt, and he was considered one of the best judo players ever.

When I entered Ishikawa's dojo for the first time, I noticed that there were three pictures strategically placed on the wall. The first picture was of Dr. Jigoro Kano, who had founded Kodokan Judo in 1882. Dr. Kano's philosophy was that judo was a system of training for the mind and body. He felt that the individual must make the most efficient use of their mental and physical energies. Dr. Kano defined the purpose

John Walters · Sensei Ishikawa · Dick Walters · Joe Walters

of judo as the development of physical strength by training one's mind and body in the technique of combat. The second picture was of Ishikawa's brother, who was a kamikaze pilot and had died during World War II. The third picture was of Ishikawa's best friend, who had also been killed in the war.

During my first training session, Ishikawa came to me and said, in broken English, "Judo will be good for you. You need not to just train your body but also your mind. I want you to just sit back and watch during your first lesson." Ishikawa was a quiet and humble man, but when I watched him work out that evening, I couldn't believe my eyes. Ishikawa was not a big person, but I was in complete awe as I watched him throw my brother around like a rag doll. He moved so smoothly that it was hard to believe that he was almost sixty years old. After the workout, Ishikawa came over and said, "When you come back, I first want you to start with mat work, and stand-up work will come later. It is very important for you to protect your leg."

I continued to work out at Ishikawa's dojo three nights a week, and during the day, I tortured myself on the Ocean City beach. At this time, it was early spring, so I had the beach all to myself. I would begin my workout by hopping thirty yards up the beach, and, in between sets, I would drop down and complete sets of push-ups. After I was warmed up, I would wear a weighted vest and continue all over again with the intervals. I did these exercises to the point of exhaustion.

I also trained at the Ocean City high school football field by walking and hopping around their track. After I reached my breaking point, I would get down on the ground and do modified gorilla walks across the field. Occasionally, people would stop and point, but I wouldn't allow them to distract me from my workout. One morning, when I was leaving the track, an older gentleman approached me and asked, "Are you a veteran?" I was hesitant to answer him, but I nodded my head and said, "Yes, I am." He immediately started to tear up and said, "I was in the army during World War II, and I saw a lot of my friends get blown to pieces. I have not seen them since they were carted off the battlefield; it is a relief to know they could have turned out just like you." I asked, "Sir, does it ever go away? I mean—the bad thoughts. I can't get it out of my mind." He thought about it for a moment and replied, "The thought of war never goes away. All you can do is just find ways to hide the pain."

By the time summer came around, I was in decent shape. One evening, after training at Ishikawa's, Dick and I decided to stop off for a beer at a bar called Tony Mart's. While we were going around the Somers Point Circle, a full can of beer bounced off our windshield. Dick then pulled into the parking lot of the Jolly Roger's Bar, and three college-age kids walked up to us. When we got out of the car, the biggest guy looked at Dick and said, "Look what we got here, three versus two. To make this fair, I will take you first." Dick smiled and replied, "No, that won't be necessary. To make this fair, I will take you and your friend over there at the same time." Dick pointed to the smallest guy and said,

"My brother will take you." Dick then turned toward me and, as he looked down at my leg, asked, "Joe, how do you feel?" I was wearing shorts, and at that point, the guy I was supposed to fight said, "This guy has a freaking wooden leg. What the hell is going on around here?" The big guy looked at Dick and said, "This is your lucky day. I think we will let you guys get out of here in one piece." Dick smiled and replied in a sarcastic tone of voice, "Thanks for sparing our lives." With that we got back in our car and drove to Tony Mart's. I think if Dick would have actually gone after those guys, I would have definitely had his back. Dick knew that I was against fighting, and if it came down to it, he would have taken all three of those guys at the same time.

The next morning, I was working out on the beach and was approached by Captain George Lafferty of the Ocean City Beach Patrol. I had been a lifeguard from 1961 through 1967, and because of my time with the Eighty-Second Airborne, Captain Lafferty had pulled for me to become a lieutenant with the beach patrol. This was the first time I had seen the captain since before the war, and when I stood up to speak with him, he said, "I heard that you have been down here every day working out. Do you miss the beach?" I replied, "Captain, it is very peaceful down here. I don't miss the beach. I miss hanging out with the guys." He smiled and said, "I have a job for you, if you're interested. I have already spoken with the mayor, and he said the job is yours for the taking. It is an office job, and I'm sure the guys will be happy to have you back." I thought about it for a moment and replied, "You know what, it will be an honor to come back and work with the men." Even though I had not yet been officially discharged from the Marine Corps, the next day I began my new job at the beach patrol headquarters. My job consisted of answering phones, talking on the radio, and helping with payroll. I would rather have been working on a lifeguard stand, but I knew that the mayor would not allow it. The work was a distraction from my thoughts of the war, and every morning I was able to row out in the ocean. This was an exercise that the average judo player did not do in training, and I was able to use it to my advantage. The hardest part of working on the beach that summer was the look on the guys' faces when they saw me without my prosthetic leg. I had to almost console people and constantly reassure them that I was all right. However, I think their attitudes quickly changed when they saw me hopping up and down the beach during my early morning torture sessions.

During that summer, I took full advantage of the Jersey Shore, specifically the Somers Point bar scene. We would begin our night at the Anchorage, Charlie's, or Gregory's. We would then go to Bay Shores or Tony Mart's, which both had live bands. There was also Diorio's and the Jolly Rogers, which were more laid-back and were good spots to relax. After the bars would close, we would end our night at the Somers Point Diner and eat a hearty breakfast in an attempt to soak up all the alcohol. This lifestyle wasn't necessarily conducive toward my training, but the summer before, I had been getting shot at in Vietnam. I had a new outlook on life, which was that "you only live once." Basically, I spent that summer training in the morning, and after work I would go home and take a quick nap. Dick and I would then drive up to Philadelphia to train with Ishikawa. After our workout, we would grab a quick bite to eat and rush back home to go out to the bars.

One night after leaving Ishikawa's club, I convinced Dick to stop off for a sandwich at a local bar in Philadelphia. This wasn't any ordinary bar. This was the place I had been thrown out of because of my veteran status. When we walked through the door and sat down at the bar, I saw the guy who had tried to fight me. The last time I saw him, I was approximately fifty pounds lighter and very weak. Now, other than the fact that I was missing my leg, my strength had returned. I was against fighting, but I felt that I needed to defend my honor and the honor of the men who I had served with in Vietnam. As I watched this guy drink shot after shot, Dick turned to me and said, "What an idiot. He keeps on staring over here. I think we should leave soon before something happens." I replied, "No, let's just stay here a little bit longer." The guy then stood up, and he was so drunk that he could barely walk. As he stumbled out the front door, I turned to Dick and said, "It's time to go."

When we walked outside, I saw the guy leaning into the driver's side window of a station wagon. There was a heavyset woman behind the wheel, who I assumed was his wife. The car was loaded with young kids, and the woman was screaming that he needed to come home. I realized at that point that this guy was not worth my time. It was actually more rewarding seeing him stumbling around completely drunk and then getting reprimanded by his wife. As Dick and I walked by, he looked at us and asked, "What are you looking at?" I thought about it for a moment and replied, "I am looking at a guy who has made some poor decisions with his life." The funny thing was that the guy didn't even reply to my comment. He just stood there watching us, and he appeared dumbfounded by what I had said.

That night, I went to the Anchorage Bar to unwind. When I sat down, I ordered their famous special, seven beers for a buck. While I was sitting there, I noticed a couple of guys staring at me. I surmised that since I was missing my leg and had a short military haircut, they assumed I was a veteran. As one of the guys walked over to me, I heard his friends say, "Do it." He then proceeded to dump a full pitcher of beer over my head and called me a baby killer. I responded by grabbing him by the neck and slamming him headfirst toward the ground. But just before he hit his head, I pulled up so he wouldn't smash his face. His friends began to gather around, and I heard one of them say, "You've done it now." However, what they didn't know was that the Anchorage was one of my favorite hangouts. I was friends not just with the owner; I was also close with the bartenders and bouncers. As I stood up to go after the next guy, the owner jumped in the middle and said, "You guys better leave be-fore you get killed." When the group of guys looked around, there were about twenty locals itching to get a piece of them. To ease the situation, I told the owner that I didn't want anyone to get hurt, and that they should be escorted outside. I'm not sure what happened once they got into the parking lot, but I'm sure the bouncers gave them what they deserved.

By this point, I had been home for less than a year, and I was constantly surrounded by chaos. People were either treating me like an invalid or looking down at me because I had fought in the war. There wasn't one night that I didn't have a bad dream about Vietnam. I also began to realize that my thoughts were eventually going to drive me over the edge. One night while training with Ishikawa, I broke down and told him what I had been going through. I was well beyond my breaking point, and I did not know what I was going to do with the rest of my life. While I was talking with him, he asked, "Were you decorated in the war?" I answered, "Yes, Sensei." He nodded his head up and down as if he wanted me to continue. He then asked, "What did you get?" I replied, "Two Purple Hearts, a Bronze Star, and a Silver Star." He asked, "What did you get them for?" I hesitated for a moment and wondered why he wanted to know. I had been presented with my medals while I was in the Philadelphia Naval Hospital, and, to be quite honest, I felt guilty accepting them. Don't get me wrong; it was an honor, but I had witnessed countless heroic acts where other Marines did not receive the recognition they deserved. I'm not sure how the rest of the military wrote up their recommendations, but I could remember watching Captain Pacello write notes on the back of a C ration box and then radioing the details into battalion. I had received my first Purple Heart during the standoff with the Viet Cong soldier, when I had been hit with grenade shrapnel. I received the Silver Star for the battle of Hill 310 and the second Purple Heart and Bronze Star for when I was wounded on September 11. Either way, I was now a highly decorated Marine, and heroes like Corporal Almanza and Private Steele had been forced to make the ultimate sacrifice.

After thinking about it for a moment, I looked at Ishikawa and replied, "Sensei, I don't know why I was awarded those medals. The Marine Corps said I went above and beyond during my course of duty, but I was actually just trying to stay alive. Those awards don't mean much, and I lost a lot of my good friends over there." Ishikawa then placed his hand on my shoulder and said, "Those medals represent the men who lost their lives while trying to fight for their country. Those medals are just like judo trophies; they're a piece of your personal history that your family can cherish forever. I understand what you are going through, and I think that it is time for you to visit Japan. My homeland will be good for your training, and I think it will help you come to terms with what you have been through."

Chapter 17 • Tokyo, Japan: Fall 1969

When I walked through the door at the Kodokan, I went directly to the office, where I met with an older Japanese gentleman. This gentleman did not speak English, and when he looked at my paperwork, he said the following three words, "Ishikawa, Walters, war." I guess it was fair to say that they were expecting me.

I went to the non-Japanese locker room, and while I was getting changed into my judo gi, several of the men were staring at my leg. As I put on my prostheses, I was very nervous and had to take a few deep breaths in order to calm down. I went upstairs to the dojo, and when I stopped to bow, approximately twenty men turned around and looked at me. These men were practicing their standing throws and were doing mat techniques that included chokes and arm bars. I felt out of place, and I didn't want to anger anyone. Therefore, my first day at the Kodokan was spent as a spectator.

I went back the following day and attended a judo class that was intended for visitors to Japan. When I entered the dojo, the main instructor came up to me and said, "You must only do mat work.

No stand up." Although this angered me, I answered, "Yes, sensei."
A short time later, another instructor who spoke fairly good English
walked up and said, "You will randori with me, and you must do
standing work." Before I could answer, he replied, "Don't worry about
him. You will work with me." While we worked out, I observed the
main instructor watching every move I made. I could tell that he was
angry because I had defied his instructions. A short time later,
he walked up to the instructor I was working with, and they began
to argue in Japanese. I'm not sure what they said to each other, but
a few minutes later, the friendly instructor walked back over and
nodded his head. He then signaled for me to get back on the mat,
and we continued with our training.

After the training session, the head instructor requested that we clean
the mats. Japanese tradition dictates that only the lower ranks do the
work, and I was the only one who was not a black belt. I grabbed a
broom, and when I started to sweep, dust flew all over the place.
A Japanese instructor then gave me a glaring look, and, shaking his
head in disgust, he shouted, "No." He then grabbed the broom out
of my hands and proceeded to show me how to sweep without raising
the dust. When I went back to sweeping, the head instructor walked
over and stopped me. He looked around the room and shouted,
"Gambare!" He pointed toward the locker room. I then lowered my
head in disgust, and while walking toward the locker room, I felt like
I had made a big mistake in coming to Japan.

I took my leg off, and when I went in to take a shower, I observed
several of the instructors soaking in a large bathtub. I tried not to make
eye contact with them, but the friendly instructor who I had trained
with earlier signaled for me to come over. While I maneuvered over,
he shouted, "Gambare!" All of the men shook their heads in agreement.
One of the men spoke very good English, and he said, "You looked
confused when you left the mat. Get in the tub. The hot water will be
good for healing your body." I was aware that it would be improper not

to wash before getting in the tub, so I lathered up with soap and poured a bucket of cold water over my body. While I was trying to climb into the tub, I reached down and touched the water. It was hot as hell, and I thought that I had burned my hand. The men laughed out loud, and it took several seconds before I was able to sit down in the tub. The English-speaking instructor then asked, "Do you know why you were told not to sweep the mats?" I answered, "No." He continued, "We study the martial arts to develop the techniques that come from the samurai. These techniques were used for combat. Today, we challenge ourselves through tournaments and fighting on the mat. You have experienced war, which is the ultimate test that any combat fighter could ever face." I asked what gambare meant, and he replied, "A true warrior who is tough and does not give up."

After the bath, I was sitting down getting dressed when one of the American students approached me and said, "I have been here for over a year, and they have never asked me to take a bath with them. All of the instructors fought in World War II, and they don't take too well to Americans. The instructor you were working out with today usually treats us the worst. For some reason, he is nice to you; the rest of us don't know why." Before I could even reply, he continued, "That son of a bitch kicks all of our butts on the mat, and it is to the point where none of us want to train with him. I don't know what you did, but he sure likes to train with you." I didn't know exactly what to say, so I replied, "My brother Dick trained with him; I guess that is why he is being nice to me." In actuality that wasn't true, and I figured that he was only treating me well because we were both war veterans.

That evening, I went to a local Japanese bar for a couple of beers. Most of the people I met were very friendly, and the bar patrons who could speak English did not hesitate to ask about my leg. A Japanese businessman, approached me and in broken English asked, "Are you an American?" I replied, "Yes, I'm from New Jersey, and I am here to train at the Kodokan." He looked down at my leg and asked, "What happened?" I replied, "I was in the war." He didn't say anything at first, but after a few seconds, he asked, "Marine Corps?" I nodded my head, and with that he mumbled a few words in Japanese and left the bar. I don't know what I said to anger him, but I decided that it would probably be in my best interest not to discuss the war with non-Americans.

As always, a few beers turned into many, and at the end of the night, I was the last one at the bar. The bartender was an older Japanese man, and when I got up to leave, he said, "You stay. We will have a drink." He poured me another beer, and when I tried to pay, he shook his head and said, "No." After he finished cleaning, he grabbed two shot glasses, a bottle of sake, and sat down next to me. As he poured our drinks, I couldn't help to think about the hangover that I was going to have the following day. The bartender did not speak much English, but after our third shot of sake, he pointed to his chest and said, "Soldier." He then pointed at me and asked, "Soldier?" I replied, "Yes, Marine." With that he poured another round of drinks.

I had been in Japan for only two days, and I already had met several men who had fought for Japan during World War II. I remembered playing war as a child, and I loved nothing more than to pretend to kill the enemy. I would fantasize about being a prisoner in a Japanese war camp or storming the beach of Normandy. Unfortunately, after experiencing war firsthand, my fantasies had now turned into dark reality. Due to a language barrier, I had very little conversation with the Japanese bartender that evening. However, after having the opportunity to speak with both American and Japanese veterans of World War II, I noticed that they all shared one common similarity. That similarly was the look in their eyes when they met another veteran. This bartender had the same look in his eyes. It could be described as pain or sorrow, but it also could be that he did not want anybody else to unlock his secrets from a long time ago.

When I awoke the following morning, I had a severe hangover. I vowed never to drink sake again. I also contemplated not going to the

Kodokan, but I knew that I could not allow alcohol to interfere with my training. When I walked into the dojo, I bowed and immediately became lightheaded. I felt like I was going to vomit. At that point, I realized that I was in no condition to work out. When I turned around to leave, I felt someone tug on my gi. It was the friendly instructor who I had worked out with the previous day, and he was signaling for me to come out onto the mat. When I walked out, he went over and spoke with a very young Japanese student. The student then walked over, bowed, and we began an hour's worth of mat work. Besides being hung over and physically exhausted, I could not believe the amount of strength this kid displayed. Even though he could have physically hurt me at any time, he was very patient and took time to correct me when I made a mistake. When we finished our workout session, I was sweating profusely, and I felt terrible. Amazingly this kid had barely broken a sweat, and he went on to fight one match after another. As I began to scurry toward the locker room, my evening of drinking was beginning to take its toll. When I finished throwing up, I turned around and was met by the friendly instructor. He looked puzzled, and before he could say anything, I blurted out, "Sake." He smiled and said, "Jack Daniels, no sake for me too. Drink water and come back out when you feel better."

As I walked back out into the dojo, one of the men yelled "sake," and everyone began to laugh. When I sat down to warm up, I saw the businessman who I had met at the bar the previous evening. I had no idea that he was a judo player, and I felt that it was important for me to apologize for whatever I had said to make him angry. When I approached him, I asked, "Did I offend you last night?" He answered, "No, sometimes I get angry when I drink. It was not your fault, and I would like to make it up to you by taking you out to dinner tonight."

I arrived at the restaurant about an hour early, so I sat at the bar and had a few beers. By the time the businessman showed up, I was already buzzed, and miraculously my hangover had dissipated. When we sat down at the table, the businessman did not waste any time and asked,

"Do you mind if we talk about the Marine Corps?" I answered, "No, I don't mind. Why do you want to know about the corps?" He replied, "My father was killed by the Marines at Iwo Jima. I have read and studied everything that I could find about the corps. I have never sat down and talked to a Marine, especially one who had fought in combat. I was a young child when he died, and I never got to know him. I am very proud that he was killed while fighting the Marines, because they are tough fighters."

That evening we talked about many different things, but the topic mostly centered on the Marine Corps. During our conversation, he signaled for the waiter and spoke to him in Japanese. A short time later, the waiter walked over and placed a bottle of sake on the table. The businessman smiled, and before he could say anything, I said, "Let's have a toast for your father and the other Japanese warriors who died at Iwo Jima." After the shot, he poured two more drinks and said, "Let's have a toast for all the brave Marines who died on the island." Without hesitating, he poured two more drinks and said, "Let's have one more toast for peace." After the bottle was finished, he stood up, saluted me, and walked out the door.

When I awoke the following morning, I was in my bed, and once again, sake had gotten the best of me. When I arrived at the Kodokan, the friendly instructor grabbed me and said, "You don't look good." I replied, "Sake." He shook his head while walking away. When I entered the dojo, the friendly instructor pointed toward the young Japanese student who I trained with the day earlier. Before I knew it, I was getting my ass kicked all over the mat. Halfway through the workout, the main instructor interrupted and said, "You want sake?" I replied, "No, sensei." He signaled for the student to take it easy on me. I surmised that I was being punished for showing up two days in a row with an obvious hangover. At the end of the day, I apologized to the nice instructor for my disrespectful behavior. After my apology, he looked at me and said, "Sake will not help you get over the war, but judo will."

During the next couple of months, I continued with my training at the Kodokan. I would begin my morning by lifting weights, which would be followed up by breathing and stretching exercises. I would then eat a small lunch and head to the Kodokan for my afternoon training session. The judo workouts were very intense, and it was not uncommon for me to lose five pounds during a session. After my judo workout was completed, I would do some calisthenics exercises and finish the day off with meditation. I'm not sure what the other wounded Vietnam veterans did to recover from the war, but Sensei Ishikawa was right. Japan was rehabilitation for not just the body but also for the mind. On weekends, I would travel into the mountains and spend the day meditating and doing yoga-type exercises. When I arrived in Japan, the war was constantly on my mind. However, after a few months, I was beginning to sleep at night without being terrorized with bad dreams. This was major progress, considering that it had been only two years since I was wounded, and by early spring, I was ready to return home.

My last night in Japan, I went to dinner with the head instructor, the nice instructor, and a few of the other judo players. While we were eating dinner, a bottle of sake was placed on the table, and everyone broke out laughing. I was then approached by the head instructor, who in my eight months in Japan had barely spoken a word to me. He asked, "How is your brother Dick?" I replied, "He is doing well, and before I arrived in Japan, I stopped off in Mexico to watch him fight in the World Games." He continued, "How did he do?" I replied, "He took fifth place, but he should have done better." The head instructor shook his head and said, "You and your brother are very tough. I hope that you take home what you have learned from the Japanese culture. Just remember, it is impossible to erase war from your memory, but you can find many ways to block it from your mind. Let judo be your way." Before I could reply, the friendly instructor came up behind me and grabbed my arm. He then said, "It is Japanese tradition to sing a song." He escorted me up onto the stage, where I was handed a microphone. I thought, "Damn, what am I going to do now." I realized that there was no way out, so I decided to sing the only song that I knew the words to: the Marine Corps hymn. I began:

From the Halls of Montezuma
To the shores of Tripoli
We fight our country's battles
In the air, on land, and sea
First to fight for right and freedom
And to keep our honor clean;
We are proud to claim the title
Of United States Marine!

The amazing thing was that as I belted out the words, all of the Japanese men attempted to sing along. Thank God they had no clue that this song was about the corps; all I could imagine was the Marines fighting at Iwo Jima and then raising the American flag at Mount Suribachi. After the song was over, the friendly instructor held my arm up into the air, and the men each grabbed a shot of sake. As they raised their glasses toward the sky, they all shouted, "Gambare!"

Chapter 18 · A Decade of Change: One-Leg Fighting

After Japan, I felt like I had finally come to terms with the hell I experienced during the war. The Japanese veterans I had trained with had all fought against the United States during World War II, and their lives had been affected forever. The crazy thing was that twenty-five years later, they helped me—an American soldier—overcome my inner demons.

When I returned to Ishikawa's dojo, I had a new outlook on life. I was also ready to move forward with my judo career. My training in Japan had provided me with the confidence that I was now ready to begin training toward competing in judo. Although I felt ready, the hardest part was convincing Sensei Ishikawa that my leg would be able to withstand the punishment of competition. When I spoke with Ishikawa about my future plans of competing, he gave me a stern look and said, "No." Before I could reply, he continued, "You will compete when I know that you're ready, physically and mentally." I respected Ishikawa's decision, not just because he was my sensei, but also because I looked up to him as a father figure. The hardest part about coming home from Vietnam was not being able to speak with my own father about my experiences at war. Even though my father could never have been replaced, Ishikawa filled a void that my brothers and I both yearned for and needed in our lives.

In April of 1971, I met my future wife, Mary Elizabeth Allen, at Tony Mart's in Somers Point. Beth was the first girl I had met since Vietnam who did not try to tell me what to do with my life. On our first date, I told her that I never planned on getting married and that my goal for the future was to travel the world doing judo. Usually these types of comments would make any woman run for the hills, but for some reason, Beth stuck around. Beth was born and raised in Osterville, Massachusetts, a little fishing village located on Cape Cod. Beth was a nurse by trade, and she was living in Ocean City with her sister, Jeanni, and her brother-in-law, David Pessano. Beth worked at the Shore Memorial Hospital in Somers Point, and on her days off, she helped out at David's store on the Ocean City boardwalk. Beth's other sister, Mardee, had also relocated to the Jersey Shore, so she was pretty content on settling down in the Ocean City area. Beth's mother, Fern, had recently passed away, and her father, Francis Allen, still lived in Osterville.

Beth's father, Francis, had served with the Army Air Corps during World War II, and he was stationed in England. Even though Francis had not experienced combat firsthand, he was very proud of the fact that he had worked on the fighter planes that were involved in all the action. One evening, Francis showed me a scrapbook that contained his discharge papers, pictures of

Francis Allen

his friends, and a meritorious Bronze Star that he had received. When he turned to the page that contained the Bronze Star, I could tell that he was hesitant showing me because of my time in Vietnam. Once he realized that I wanted to look, a big smile crept across his face, and he said, "We lost a lot of planes that were piloted by the best in the Army Air Corps. It was hard not to get close to those guys, because they were larger than life. When they did not return, it affected everyone on the base." He pointed to a picture and said, "One night, I was out drinking with these guys at a local pub, and I got really drunk. On my way back to the barracks, I cut through a cow pasture, and I must have fallen down into a pile of manure. When I got back to my bunk, all the men were yelling at me, and I had to be physically carried into the shower. The next day, I awoke not remembering what had happened, but I was quickly reminded when I asked my bunk mate why the room smelled like crap."

Beth's father was a good man, but I don't think he necessarily knew how to deal with me. I was seven years older than his daughter, and it was obvious that I had no intentions of settling down. It also didn't help that Beth was a free spirit, and the combination of the two was probably very frustrating to him. But deep down, I think Francis knew that I had only good intentions toward his daughter, and eventually he warmed up to me. It probably also helped that he remarried a wonderful woman named Marion Wolsieffer, and she and I hit it off right from the start. Although Marion could never replace their mother, I know that Beth and her sisters were relieved that their father had found someone to grow old with.

In the fall of 1971, Beth and I traveled to Germany and Holland, where I had the privilege to train at several different judo schools. The one thing I noticed about the Europeans was the amount of upper body strength they displayed. The Japanese utilized more of their legs and core body strength, while the Europeans were physically strong, which enabled them to use their upper body to dominate an opponent. While in Holland, I trained with Jon Bluming, who had fought with the Van Heutz regiment during the Korean War. Jon had been wounded in battle, and while rehabilitating in Japan, he was introduced to judo during a visit to the Kodokan. Jon was an excellent teacher, and from his instruction, I was able to blend together the European and Japanese styles and mold them into my own unique type of fighting.

After Europe, Beth and I returned to Ocean City, and I continued my intense training regimen. During this time, I also began to fight in local judo tournaments. Even though I had always trained with my prosthetic leg, it didn't take long for my opponents to discover my weaknesses. Therefore, I was easily beat in all of my matches, and the frustration of losing made me question my own fighting ability. I had also become distracted during my training sessions, and it got to the point where one evening, Ishikawa approached me and said, "When you started to compete, I didn't say a word because you knew how I felt. Physically, you are ready for competition, but mentally you're not quite there. Without the two together, you cannot be successful in judo." I asked, "Sensei, what do you think I should do?" He thought about it for a couple of seconds and answered, "You need to take a break from competing, and I think it is time for you to return to Japan."

In 1973, I returned to Tokyo to continue my training at the Kodokan. During this time, I had the opportunity to work out with Isao Okano, who had won the gold medal for Japan during the 1964 Olympic Games. Besides being an outstanding judo player, Okano was an excellent teacher who went out of his way to help his students. Okano would often imitate the way that I moved by keeping his left leg totally straight in an attempt to mimic my prosthetic leg. By doing this, Okano was able to develop several throws that I could implement in my training and eventually use in competition. After a few months with Okano, I noticed that my overall strength and judo ability had greatly improved. My mind was clear, and I think Okano's teaching was just another piece of the puzzle in developing my judo skills.

While in Japan, I also met an American named Bill Sanford, who urged me to come to Houston, Texas, and train at the Karl Geis Judo Academy. Bill and a few of the other judo players were planning on spending the entire year training for the 1975 United States Judo Nationals. By this point in my life, I had traveled all across the world studying judo, but I had never trained at any American dojo besides Ishikawa's. It was not that I was tired of Ishikawa or the Jersey Shore, but I think I was ready for a change with my life. Since Vietnam, I had been living off my Marine Corps retirement, which meant that my college education was basically going to waste. I decided that if I did go to Houston, this would be a great place for me to begin my career as a schoolteacher.

When I returned from Japan, my first course of business was visiting Sensei Ishikawa. When I entered his dojo, Ishikawa smiled and asked, "How was Japan?" I answered, "It was great. I am thinking about going to Texas to train with Karl Geis. I met a few guys in Japan who live in Houston, and while out there, I am even thinking about pursuing a career as a schoolteacher." He nodded his head and said, "Karl Geis is a good instructor, and I think it is a good idea for you to travel and train at different dojos. I also got word back from the Kodokan about your training sessions with Okano. I am very proud of you, and I think it is now time for you to begin gearing yourself toward competing at a serious level."

In September of 1974, I began my teaching career at the Dogan Elementary School, which was located in the Fifth Ward District of Houston, Texas. On the morning of my first day, my stump opened up, and I was unable to wear my prosthetic leg. When the fifth grade students first walked into the classroom and saw me standing there with only one leg, you could have heard a pin drop. While the kids got settled into their seats, they were all staring at me. I knew that I had to break the ice, so I began by saying to the class, "Your first assignment is to guess what happened to my leg. Does anyone have any ideas?" At first, the students just sat there with dumbfounded looks on their faces, but they quickly perked up when a kid in the first row blurted out, "Shark attack." I replied, "No." And as I smiled, all of the kids started to laugh. The students then all at once raised their hands, and I heard the following responses: dog bite, car accident, bear attack, plane crash, and gunshot wound. I answered, "You are all wrong; I was actually abducted by aliens, and when the spaceship dropped me off in the woods, Bigfoot ate my leg." As the entire room erupted in laughter, I held up a magazine article that was written about the Vietnam War. With that, I began my first lesson as a public schoolteacher by stating, "I am a Vietnam veteran, and I was shot during the war." I don't know if this was the proper way to start off as a teacher, but I was able to immediately grab the attention of the students, which in turn made it a very enjoyable and rewarding school year.

Besides teaching school, I spent all my time at the Karl Geis Judo Academy. Sensei Geis was one hell of an instructor, and his training techniques were comparable to what I had learned during my time in Japan and Europe. After about one month of training, Sensei Geis approached me and said, "Joe, I think it is time to promote you to black belt." This was a great honor, but I knew that Sensei Ishikawa did not want me promoted until I was absolutely ready. I thanked Sensei Geis for the recommendation, and I answered, "Sir, I don't think that I am ready yet." He replied, "I will respect your wishes, but the next time I bring up this matter, you will be promoted."

During that winter, I fought in the 1975 Judo Districts. Basically, if I placed in this tournament, I would be able to fight in the spring at the US Judo Nationals. When I arrived at the districts, the first thing I did was find out who I would be competing against. The judo player I was going to face was a tough competitor, but I had noticed a weakness of his when I saw him fight in an earlier tournament. I observed that when he was on the ground, he would allow his opponents to come in on top, and then he would suddenly turn them over. By doing this, he would end up in the pinning position and then eventually win the match. When our match began, I threw him and immediately maneuvered into mat work. I pretended that I was coming in high, hoping that he would allow me to get in real close. Fortunately, my plan worked, and at the very last moment, I dropped my hips, got on top of him, and pinned him for the win. Finally, I had won a match, and in doing so, I had qualified to fight in the nationals. After the tournament, Sensei Geis shook my hand and said, "Joe, you did an outstanding job, and you're now a black belt."

Shortly after the districts, I proposed marriage to Beth, but I had one stipulation. I knew that since I had a large family, who mostly lived in New Jersey, that a wedding could cause a lot of turmoil between our families. Therefore, when I gave Beth the ring, I told her that my offer of marriage was good for only a few weeks. Exactly three weeks later, Billy Sanford stood as my best man as Beth and I walked down the aisle. I'm sure it wasn't the fairytale wedding that Beth had always dreamed of, but for the first time since Vietnam, I had broken a promise. That promise was when I told Beth on our first date that I was never getting married. I never intended on getting married because I had never met anyone quite like Beth. Beth had always gone out of her way to take care of me, and during the time we spent in Europe, I realized that we were meant to spend the rest of our lives together. What made our marriage even less traditional was the fact that we spent our honeymoon at the 1975 US Judo National Senior Championships in California. I had trained for approximately one year for this tournament, and I knew that I was ready to fight.

When I stepped out onto the mat, I bowed toward my opponent and took one step forward, which let the referee know that I was ready to fight. The referee waived his hands in a manner that indicated a negative response, and he signaled for me to immediately exit the mat. He continued to point for me to leave, but I adamantly refused. At that point, Billy Sanford ran out onto the mat, and he began to argue with the official. I heard the referee say, "His prosthetic leg doesn't even move, which gives him an advantage. He should have been disqualified at the districts, so he doesn't even deserve to be here." Billy continued, "He won fair and square, so he is entitled to fight in this tournament." After approximately a half hour of arguing, I was finally allowed to fight. Either way, I guess it didn't really matter because I lost the match on a decision that was given by the referee. I may not have won my match, but I did receive the Inspiration Award, which was voted on by the other competitors. This was a great honor, but I was unable to receive this award because when it was presented, I was sitting in a bar with Billy Sanford. By that point, I was probably on my third or fourth beer. I had lost my match, but I became the first person in the history of judo to fight in the US nationals with a disability. This was a major accomplishment, considering that I was almost disqualified because of my prosthetic leg.

In the summer of 1975, Beth and I returned to New Jersey for good. By this point, my brother Dick had opened Walters Judo School, located on the corner of Ninth and Asbury in Ocean City. Although I continued to train in Philadelphia with Ishikawa, most of my workouts were conducted at Dick's school. I was also hired as an eighth grade teacher at the Dennis Township Elementary School in Cape May County. The teaching experience I had garnered in Houston definitely gave me the confidence to teach without the use of a prosthetic leg. Of course, the first day of school was filled with a million questions about my leg, but after a while, the kids moved on to another topic. I guess you could say that for the average eighth-grader, the fact that their teacher had only one leg was not that newsworthy.

When I arrived at the 1976 Judo Districts, I was pulled aside by several judo officials. I was informed that the US Judo Executive Committee had decided that I was no longer allowed to fight with the use of a prosthetic leg. While I was standing there in total shock, I turned to my brother John and said, "My judo career is over before it even began. What am I supposed to do now?" John then looked at one of the officials and said, "I know what you're going to do: you're going to compete in

Joe Walters with Tournament Trophy

this tournament." The main official interrupted, "I don't think you understand; your brother is not allowed to fight with a prosthetic leg." John replied, "All right, he will fight without it." The officials looked at each other, and the main official said, "It is impossible for him to fight with one leg. Even if he could, your brother could get hurt." At that point, John and the officials went into a back room and had a private meeting to discuss if I was going to be able to fight. I'm not sure what was said during the private meeting, but after approximately twenty minutes of negotiating, John walked out of the room and said, "Start warming up, because you're going to fight." I asked, "With one leg?" John answered, "Yeah, with one leg. I know that you have never done judo without your prosthetic leg, but there has to be a first time for everything."

That afternoon, I began a new chapter of my life: competing in judo with one leg. When I hopped out onto the mat for the first match, my opponent looked at me and asked, "Are you serious?" I didn't answer him, and when I heard the referee say "hajime," which means "begin" in Japanese, I blacked out. I don't remember what exactly happened, but somehow I had won the very first match that I had ever fought with one leg. Even though I got my ass kicked during my next two matches, I had qualified for the nationals, and I knew that the next few years of judo were going to be very interesting.

Chapter 19 · The Motivating Force: July 4, 1978

As I sat on the beach and stared at the sky, I wondered where the past ten years had gone. It had been a decade since Vietnam, and during this time, my life had changed significantly. Besides getting married, I was now the father of a fourteen-month-old daughter, Alison, and newborn son, Joe. Even though my wife and children had created a constant stability in my life, I was unsure of what was in store for my judo career. I had been easily defeated during the 1976, 1977, and 1978 US Judo National Championships. After those three years of intense training sessions, which were followed by disappointing losses, I was contemplating retiring from competition for good.

While sitting on the beach, my daughter knocked over a full bottle of soda, which spilled all over our blanket. As my wife was cleaning up the mess, I must have been distracted, because I did not hear when the first wave of fireworks shot off into the air. However, when I heard the explosion that followed, my mind jumped back to Vietnam, and the voices of my friends who had died under my command flashed through my mind.

"Keep on moving and get up that hill. Lieutenant, what are we going to do? They're starting to come into our perimeter. I need ammo! I have been hit! I need a corpsman! Lieutenant, I can't go any farther. Help me, please, help me! Don't leave me here! I want my mom! Make it stop! Make the pain stop! Corpsman! I want to go home! I need ammo! Help me! I don't want to die!"

And then I heard:

"Don't quit! Don't give up! You can do it! You have it in you! It's yours for the taking! You've worked hard for this! You have to go on! You must go on! You can't stop now! Do it for us! Do it for us, Lieutenant! Do it for us!"

"Joe, are you all right? Joe! Joe, what is wrong? Speak to me, Joe. Are you OK?" When I finally snapped out of it, I was sweating profusely, and I answered, "Beth, I am fine." She continued, "What is wrong with you?" I answered, "The fireworks brought back some painful memories, but I now know what I have to do." Beth shrugged her shoulders and asked, "And what is that?" I replied, "I have to win the nationals. Not for me, but for the men. The men who died helping me. The men I let down. The men I couldn't save. The men who never made it home."

The next day, I began a new training regimen that doubled the intensity of my past workouts. Since Vietnam, I had always trained at an intense level. However, I knew that if I wanted to take the next step toward winning the nationals, I had to make some serious changes to my past workouts. Therefore, I set up a yearlong training program that emphasized one competition in particular: the 1979 US National Judo Masters Championships.

From July 5 to December 24 of 1978, I trained the hardest that I had ever trained in my life. I did everything from hopping sprints on the beach, hill training with a weighted vest, throwing large rocks across my front yard, to doing mat work to the point of complete exhaustion. For strength, I picked the following four exercises that complemented my fighting style: incline bench press, approximately twenty-five to fifty reps per set; hammer pulls (heavy weight), four sets of ten to fifteen reps; one-arm bridges from supine position with heavy weight; box carries, hopping while holding weights in front of the body.

During my workouts with Ishikawa, he had me practice countless reps of bridges and lifting exercises. While ground fighting, there are certain situations where you are just trying to create a small space between you and your opponent. Once that space is created, your main priority is to get your hands in the right position. Most of the time, your hands are locked in place, which prevents you from being able to extend your arms out. Therefore, bridging and lifting creates that gap, and by using your rotational muscles, you can quickly turn over your opponent and go in for the pin.

From January 1 to April of that year, my goal was mostly to maintain my strength and above all my endurance. I was afraid of burning out too soon, and by February of 1979, I had lost ten pounds. However, my overall strength had improved. For the first time, I was confident in my ability, and I knew that I was ready to go all the way.

I arrived in California several days before the 1979 nationals, and I took that time to focus on gearing down my training. I did a lot of walking, light weightlifting, and some exercises inside the hotel pool. Most importantly, I had to monitor my food intake, because if I weighed in too heavy, I would not have been allowed to fight.

The Thursday before the competition, I officially made weight during registration. So that evening, I met a few friends at the hotel bar to have dinner and a few beers. When I entered the restaurant, I ran into Hayward Nishioka, who asked, "How is your brother Dick doing?" I answered, "The same as always. Even though he is retired from competing, he still trains as hard as ever." Nishioka smiled and said, "Everyone knows how hard Dick trains, and there were a lot of guys in the heavyweight division who were relieved when he retired. Dick was tough."

When I sat down at the table with my friends, they were all looking at me, and one of them asked, "How the hell do you know Hayward Nishioka? He is a judo legend." Before I could answer, a judo player who was new to the sport asked, "Who is Nishioka?"

Hayward Nishioka was a three-time US national judo champion, a member of four US international teams, and in 1966 a gold medalist at the British Colombian Championships. Nishioka was also a Pan American champion, and he took fifth place at both the 1965 and 1967 World Judo Championships. Besides being a tough competitor, he was recognized as an International Judo Federation Class A referee and a US Class A coach.

After dinner, the rest of the guys turned in for the evening. However, like always, I remained at the bar. While talking with a fellow judo player, he asked, "Did you check and see who you're going to fight? I always look, because I want to see how many men are in my pool and find out who I will be going against in my first match." I answered, "No way, I don't like to know. I will sleep better tonight not knowing. On Saturday morning I'll look, then try to come up with a game plan. I find that I do best if I have time to observe my first opponent. I especially like to watch him during his warm-up routine." The player then asked, "How does that help you?" I replied, "I try to figure out what throws he may like to use. If he is short and stocky, he may favor certain techniques, while a taller competitor may have a different style of fighting. But no matter how much I mentally prepare before a match, it seems like all of my strategy just goes out the window when I hop out onto the mat."

Chapter 20 · Strength in Numbers

When I entered the locker room, I sat down to take off my prosthetic leg, and I could feel the stares from the other competitors. When I took off my leg, I could see several men whispering to each other, but I tried not to let it bother me. At that moment, some change fell out of my pocket and dropped all over the ground. When I reached down to grab it, several of the men rushed over to help. I said, "Thank you guys, but I got it." As I was picking up the loose change, I noticed that one of the men was still standing there. When I looked up, he said, "Joe, I just want you to know that I think what you're doing is great. My brother died in Vietnam, and I know that he would have been very proud of you." I replied, "Thank you." Then I went back to preparing for the competition.

My preparation began by placing a large sock over my stump and then a leather shell that was hooked onto a belt. After the leather piece was secured to the stump, it took at least one roll of duct tape to keep the contraption in place. As I was taping up my leg, I overheard a few of the guys talking about my past. I heard one man say to the other, "That's Dick Walters's brother over there. He was in the Marine Corps, and he lost his leg while fighting in Vietnam. Can you believe that after everything he has been through, the US judo officials told him that he is no longer allowed to use a prosthetic leg during competitions? You have to give the man a lot of credit, but how good can he be fighting with only one leg? It is impossible, and if you ask me, I think he is just setting himself up for one giant letdown." The other guy replied, "Impossible? Maybe, but don't forget that he is a Walters."

As I was sitting there, I wanted to turn around and say something, but I knew that I couldn't take out eleven years of frustration on them. It was disheartening because it seemed like most people felt sorry for me because of my disability, and I was not taken seriously as a competitor. I was missing a leg, but I had come to terms with my situation a long time ago, and I just wished by now that everyone else would have done the same.

I left the locker room and used my crutches to get out into the main arena. In an attempt to hide from the audience, I sat behind the auditorium bleachers and began to stretch out. I had trained for the last year, and even though I was physically ready, I was still mentally dealing with the war. A short time later, I checked in with the registration table and found out who I would be fighting for my first match. I was familiar with this competitor, and when I saw him warming up in the corner of the gym, I went over to speak with him. As I approached, I heard him say to another judo player, "There is no way that I am going to get pinned by this guy." I turned around before he noticed me and went back behind the bleachers to warm up.

The announcer called my name, and when I hopped out onto the main arena, I could hear the roar of the crowd. My opponent stepped onto the mat, and prior to fighting, we both bowed toward each other. As I looked up, I felt like I was having a panic attack, and I was worried that I was going to pass out. I signaled to the referee that I needed a couple of seconds to gather my composure, and I bent over to catch my breath. As I lifted up my head, I noticed an Oriental man sitting in the audience. We made eye contact, and at that very moment, my mind flashed back to another time and place.

When I snapped back to reality, I scanned the crowd, but the Oriental man was gone. The referee asked, "Are you all right?" But I was still in shock that the last eleven years of my life had flashed through my mind in a matter of seconds. I was beginning to catch my breath, and when I looked back into the crowd, our eyes met once again. At that point, I realized why seeing this man had set my mind racing into the first flashback I had since the fireworks show on the Fourth of July. This gentleman looked exactly like the Vietnamese soldier who I had encountered during the brief standoff where I was wounded with grenade shrapnel. Even though I had not thought about this incident for years, I remembered that shortly after my return from Vietnam, I was haunted with bad dreams about how this encounter could have turned out. Fortunately for the both of us, these nightmare outcomes never occurred.

I then signaled to the referee that I was ready to fight, and at that point, I remembered what my opponent had said before the match: "There is no way that I am going to get pinned by this guy." With that comment freshly etched into my mind, I hopped toward my opponent, and when the referee shouted "Hajime!" I said, "It is on now."

During the match, my opponent spent a considerable amount of time just trying to avoid getting close to me. I noticed that when he was near the edge of the mat, he would often pivot his body to avoid stepping out of bounds. Consequently, by doing this, his legs were forced to open up, which in turn weakened his balance. I began my attack by forcing him toward the edge of the mat, and when he started to pivot, I attempted ouchigari, which is a leg throw, by hooking and reaping his left leg. When I made the hook, he stepped back with his right foot, and at that point, I reached down and grabbed his left heel. I then forced my body toward his and knocked him to the ground. When he hit the mat, I jumped up on top and pinned him to win the match.

At the beginning of my second match, my opponent immediately came in for a hip throw. I countered him with a tani-otoshi (valley drop), and he landed on his side. When I went in for the pin, he countered by rolling over onto his stomach. I then maneuvered onto his upper back and slipped my hand under his chin for a neck choke. After a few seconds, he tapped out. For the first time in my judo career, I had won two matches in a row, and I would now be fighting for first place.

While standing on the edge of the mat, a couple of judo players approached me, and one of them asked, "Walters, do you know who you are fighting?" I shrugged my shoulders, and when they all started to laugh, I asked, "Who?" I almost fell over when one of them answered, "Hayward Nishioka."

As I stood there in complete shock, an idea flashed through my mind: "He won't expect me to try and throw him as soon as I have one grip." As I pictured this technique in my mind, I remembered Sensei Ishikawa making me practice this one-arm Yoko-wakare throw. As I thought back, it was as if Ishikawa knew all along that the outcome of the biggest match of my life could be decided by a very unconventional judo throw.

As I watched Nishioka walk out toward the mat, I heard my name being called out by several spectators in the crowd. When I looked in their direction, I saw the entire Marine Corps judo team sitting in the balcony section of the auditorium. These guys were going nuts, and several of them were shouting, "Ooh rah!" and "Semper fi!" I had never seen such a rowdy crowd at a judo tournament, let alone a crowd that was rooting against Nishioka, who was one of the best judo players in the world. I could tell that the officials were becoming aggravated because of all the noise, but what could you expect from a bunch of hardcore Marines? Even though these guys were causing quite a disturbance, their presence had a calming effect on me. I was no longer nervous, and for the first time since Vietnam, I was reunited with my Marine Corps brothers. To say the least, I was ready to fight.

The announcer said, "We have Joe Walters from New Jersey, and
we have Hayward Nishioka from California. Hayward is a three-time
national champion." At that point, the referee motioned for us to enter
the mat area. In the background, I could still hear the announcer
talking about Nishioka's achievements in judo. I hopped out onto the
mat, and when I came face to face with Nishioka, we bowed toward
each other. We both took one step forward, and at that moment, the
referee shouted, "Hajime!" As we maneuvered toward each other,
I could still hear the announcer talking about Nishioka. "In 1966 he
won a gold medal at the British Colombian Championships, and one
year later, he won the gold at the 1967 Pan American Games." As
Nishioka took several steps toward me, I hopped once, and at that
moment, we both got our one-handed grip. From past experience,
I learned that many judo players would wait for me to reach for my
second grip. Once I reached, they would try to throw me with a forward
throw, especially because I had only one leg, and my balance would
be broken in that direction. As I pretended to reach for my second grip,
I immediately jumped in and tried to throw him with Yoko-wakare,
which is a sacrifice throw. In judo, a sacrifice is when you throw yourself
to the ground on purpose, which allows your momentum in conjunction
with your hands and feet to throw your opponent on his back.

Nishioka was able to stop my throw by driving me down with his
hands, bending his knees, and slightly leaning into me with his body.
Since his hands were almost fully extended, I attempted an arm bar.
To counter this move, Nishioka bent down, and while he leaned into
me, his hips slightly rose off of the mat. Upon seeing this, I slid under
him, and while doing a bridge-and-lift technique, I turned Nishioka
onto his back, and I landed directly on top of him.

For several seconds, I didn't realize what had happened until I heard
my Marine comrades shouting, "Hold him! You got him! Pin him!
Don't let him breathe!" Due to all the confusion, I wasn't even aware
that I was in the ideal position for a pin. I grabbed Nishioka with a

kuzure kami shiho gatame, which is a variant upper four-direction hold. I didn't know how he was going to react, so I squeezed him with every ounce of strength that I had. I also kept my hips low just in case I had to counter one of his moves. I was waiting for him to push into me and try to move away or attempt a bridge-and-lift technique. Once I had a strong grip, I decided that my main focus would be to stop him from lifting his hips. I hoped that this might prevent him from turning and twisting in order to gain the momentum that he would need to escape. While Nishioka attempted to bridge and maneuver away from me, I was beginning to lose my grip. My game plan was to squeeze him with all of my might and just hope for the best. At that moment, I could hear the Marines shouting, "Hold him! Don't let him get away! Keep your hips down!" It was really noisy, and I had never experienced anything like that in my life. The guys were really excited, and I just hoped that I wouldn't let them down. As the Marines shouted words of encouragement, I thought about the first time I had heard the phrase "strength in numbers." I had just arrived in Vietnam, and a war-stricken lieutenant I met at the An Hoa base camp said this phrase to me. At the time, I didn't fully comprehend the meaning of this saying, but now I understood.

The Marines who I had served with in Vietnam not only helped me survive the battlefield, but they showed me the true meaning of being part of a brotherhood. After I was wounded and lost my leg, it was my own family who had helped me through the transition from being a wounded soldier to being able to function in everyday life. The Japanese soldiers who I had trained with while in Japan showed me that in order to move on from the horrors of war, I had to forgive the enemies of my past. Now, as I was on the verge of beating one of the best judo players of all time, it was the Marines in the upper balcony displaying strength in numbers, pushing me past my breaking point, and providing me with the extra strength I needed to hold down Nishioka.

This turn of events had happened so fast that while I was trying to pin Nishioka, I could hear the announcer still talking about his past judo accomplishments. The announcer was mentioning how he had placed fifth in the World Games on two separate occasions, and with that, I heard the announcer shout, "I don't believe it! Walters is holding down Nishioka! Walters is holding down Nishioka! I can't believe what I am seeing here. Somebody should call the newspapers or something. I can't believe it."

The timekeeper then threw a beanbag onto the mat, which signaled to the referee that I had won the match. With that the announcer continued to shout, "He won! The match is over! Walters beat Nishioka! Walters beat Nishioka! I can't believe it!" I couldn't see the beanbag, so I continued to hold on until I heard the referee say, "The match is over." The crowd was going crazy, and the guys from the Marine Corps judo team were hugging each other and jumping all around. As I hopped up to the starting position, the referee signaled that I was the winner. I looked over toward Nishioka, and I noticed that he was slowly getting up off the ground. Once on his feet, Nishioka walked over, stood on his mark, and the referee raised his hand toward me and said, "Ippon." We bowed, shook hands, and we both left the mat without saying a word to each other.

During the award ceremony, it was actually Nishioka who reached his hand out to assist me while I was hopping up onto the first place podium. As I was presented with my trophy, Nishioka turned to me and said, "We must meet again."

Chapter 21 · My Father

When my father finished saying the words we must meet again, I
looked at him and asked, "Did you guys ever fight again?" My father
laughed and replied, "No, thank God. I could have faced Nishioka
a hundred more times, and I'm sure that match would have been my
only win. Nishioka was one of the best judo competitors of all time,
but on that day, it was my time to shine. All of the cards were in my
favor, and I prevailed. As a result, a new chapter in my life began, and
I could finally put the past behind me. On that day, a Vietnam veteran
with one leg, who most called handicapped, was the best. And no one
could feel sorry for me ever again or doubt my judo ability—I had
proved everyone wrong. It was that simple. People now had to take
me seriously. Deep down, I was so relieved because I could now put
the war behind me. Not only had I won the judo match, but I had also
gained the confidence to live the rest of my life without ever doubting
myself. I did it, I accomplished it, and I have never looked back."

I was in complete awe that my father had divulged a part of his life
story that spanned an eleven-year time frame. His story began with him
entering Vietnam as a twenty-seven-year-old Marine and leaving three

months later as a permanently disabled veteran. It concluded with him becoming a schoolteacher and, above all, an accomplished judo player. Growing up, I had always known about his accomplishments in judo, but I never knew what had happened during the middle portion of those eleven years. I was honored that he had shared this part of his life with me. At that moment, though, I began to feel guilty about one thing in particular. I asked

him, "Does it bother you that I never carried on the Walters family judo tradition?" My father smiled and answered, "No, that was your sister Alison's job. She has been the only family member since your uncles to become a black belt, and she has kept the tradition alive. I am very proud of her accomplishments, and she has become an excellent judo teacher. But concerning you, I have always had other plans." I asked, "What?" My father replied, "In due time, you will realize it on your own."

George Harris · Joe Walters

The process of writing this book has helped me to understand many things about my father, especially what the sport of judo has done for his life. After the war, I think he used judo to camouflage what he experienced during combat. It was as if judo was his own personal therapy, and it enabled him to stay focused on improving physically and mentally. Judo also distracted others, drawing their focus away from his one leg and the hell he went through in Vietnam. Most of the time, people were more intrigued by how he was actually able to do judo at all. I guess it was a great smokescreen while it lasted, but I could be fooled for only so long. I was determined to learn everything about him, and thank God I did. My father is and always will be an inspiration to others. Although he is not perfect, he has made me the man that I am today: an honest man, a good husband, and a great father. And besides being an inspiration, my father became one hell of a judo competitor.

After becoming the 1979 US Judo National Masters Champion, he received the Mid Atlantic AUU Outstanding Athlete Award for the sport of judo. The most impressive thing about that ceremony was the presence of a young man who had won the track and field award—Carl Lewis. At the time, he was the top-ranked high school track athlete in the country. Extraordinarily, my father and Carl Lewis had one thing in common: after 1979, each man became very successful in his sport. Carl Lewis went on to become a nine-time Olympic gold medalist and is considered one of the greatest athletes of all time. Though my father could never be truly compared to Carl Lewis, he didn't do so badly for himself, either. Listed below are his judo accomplishments:

1980: First place at the US Judo National Masters Championships

1981: Third place at the US Judo National Masters Championships

1982: First place at the US Judo National Masters Championships

1983: First place at the US Judo National Masters Championships

1984: First place at the US Judo National Masters Championships

1985: Third place at the US Judo National Masters Championships

1986: First place at the US Judo National Masters Championships

1987: First place at the US Judo National Masters Championships; first judo recipient of the Vince Lombardi Award for Outstanding Athlete

1990: First place at the US Judo National Masters Championships

1994: Second place at the World Masters Games in Australia

1995: Retired from judo competition

George Harris · Joe Walters

In 2003, my father emerged from eight years of retirement and returned to fight at the Kodokan in Tokyo, Japan, during the World Masters Games. He won only one match out of three, but he was able to officially retire from competition at the Kodokan, which was where it all began.

In closing, I have realized through this experience—especially learning about my father and writing his story—that my own achievements have been made possible only because of what he endured, as if he used his life experiences, good and bad, to teach me about the concept of strength in numbers. And now, thanks to the lessons I learned from him, I am teaching my own daughter about these concepts, and I know that she will pass on my father's legacy to her children someday.

As it stands, my father, Joe Walters, is in his early seventies, and he is still tough as nails. He works out twice a day and continues to train and teach judo. Every day I spend with him is a gift, and I'm fortunate to have such a smart father. And when I say smart, I mean a genius;

I don't know how he did it. When he told me that he always had other plans for me, I wasn't sure what he meant. But somehow, he tricked his own son, a guy who also struggled in school, into writing a book about him. Don't get me wrong—it has been a real privilege to tell his life story, and I hope I was able to capture his true nature: a man who was able to use the strength of others to overcome great hardship. And even though I am still a huge fan of Pete Rose, Rambo, and Chuck Norris, my father will forever be my hero.

The End

Author's Biography

Joseph F. Walters resides in Upper Township, New Jersey with his wife and young daughter. This book is about his father, Joe Walters.

CPSIA information can be obtained at www.ICGtesting.com
Printed in the USA
LVOW08s2148030615

441126LV00016B/451/P